TOWER HAMLETS COLLEGE
Learning Centre

078848

The Advanced Study Series

D1081277

P1 Improving Skills

THE LIBRARY
TOWER HAMLETS COLLEGE
POPLAR HIGH STREET
LONDON E14 0AF
Tel: 0207 510 7763

by
Shaun Armstrong and Chris Huffer

Solomon
Press

Published by Solomon Press Limited
3, Dunkirk Business Park
Frome Road
Southwick
Wiltshire. BA14 9NL

Tel: 01225 775078
E-mail: info@solomon-press.com
Website: www.solomon-press.com

The *Advanced Study Series* is a trade mark of Solomon Press

© S Armstong C Huffer 2001
First published 2001

ISBN 1901724 15 8

All rights reserved.
No part of this publication may be reproduced,
stored in a retrieval system, or transmitted in any
form or by any means without the prior
written permission of Solomon Press.

Order No:

Class: 510·076 ARM

Accession No: 078848

Type: L

Design and typesetting by S Armstrong and Pedeke Ltd, Bridgwater,
Somerset.
Printed in Great Britain by Friary Print Ltd, Dorchester, Dorset.

CONTENTS

GCSE Skills Review

Exercise 1S   Skills Practice

1   Write down all the factors of

    a 9   **b** 14   **c** 24   **d** 41   **e** 60   **f** 250

2   Find the highest common factor of

    a 8 and 12   **b** 21 and 35   **c** 36, 60 and 108

3   Find the lowest common multiple of

    a 7 and 5   **b** 28 and 42   **c** 8, 12 and 20

4   List the prime numbers between 50 and 60.

5   Guards A, B and C each patrol one wing of a prison. To complete one patrol takes guard A 10 minutes, guard B 15 minutes and guard C 25 minutes.

At 1 pm the three guards set off from their base, O, and patrol their respective wings continuously throughout the afternoon.

    a Find how long it takes before guards A and B are again at O together.

    b Find the time at which guards B and C next see each other at O.

    c Find the first time after 1 pm at which all three guards are again at O together.

6   Evaluate

    a $\frac{1}{3}+\frac{1}{3}$ **b** $\frac{3}{8}+\frac{1}{2}$ **c** $\frac{1}{5}+\frac{3}{10}$ **d** $\frac{5}{8}-\frac{1}{4}$ **e** $\frac{2}{5}\times\frac{1}{3}$ **f** $\frac{3}{7}\div\frac{2}{3}$

7   Express as a mixed number

    a $\frac{3}{2}$ **b** $\frac{7}{4}$ **c** $\frac{11}{3}$ **d** $\frac{17}{6}$ **e** $\frac{21}{5}$ **f** $\frac{61}{8}$

8   Express as an improper fraction

    a $2\frac{1}{2}$ **b** $2\frac{1}{4}$ **c** $1\frac{4}{7}$ **d** $3\frac{3}{4}$ **e** $5\frac{2}{5}$ **f** $11\frac{3}{8}$

9   Evaluate

    a $\frac{2}{3}+\frac{3}{4}$ **b** $2\frac{3}{8}+1\frac{3}{4}$ **c** $2\frac{5}{8}-1\frac{3}{16}$

    d $3\frac{1}{4}\times\frac{2}{3}$ **e** $4\frac{2}{5}\div\frac{3}{5}$ **f** $5\frac{1}{4}\div3\frac{3}{8}$

10   A set of drills range in diameter from $\frac{1}{16}$ of an inch to $\frac{3}{8}$ of an inch, in steps of $\frac{1}{64}$ of an inch.

    a Find the diameter of the drill which lies between $\frac{1}{4}$ and $\frac{9}{32}$ of an inch.

    b Find the diameter of the middle drill when they are arranged in order of size.

11 Given that y is directly proportional to x, and that when $x = 7.2$, $y = 5.4$, calculate the value of y when $x = 3$.

12 Given that y is inversely proportional to x, and that when $x = 3$, $y = 4$, calculate the value of x when $y = 4.8$

13 Given that y is directly proportional to x^2, and that when $x = 8$, $y = 25.6$, calculate the value of y when $x = 3.5$

14 Calculate the length x in each case.

a

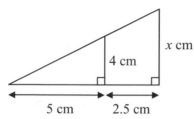

b

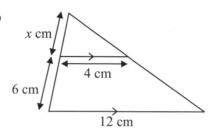

15 A scale model is made of a museum building, the shape of which is a cylinder. The volume of the building is $14\,000$ m^3 and the area of its base is $1\,750$ m^2.

    a Calculate the height of the building.

    Given that the height of the model is to be 32 cm,

    b find the ratio of the dimensions of the model to the dimensions of the building,

    c find the volume of the scale model.

16 Write each of the following in the form 3^k.

    a $3^2 \times 3^5$ **b** $3 \times 3^4 \times 3^{11}$ **c** $3^8 \times 3^{-3}$ **d** $3^{13} \div 3^6$

17 Write in standard form

    a $5\,320\,000$ **b** 237.6 **c** 0.003 **d** $0.000\,018\,3$

18 Write as ordinary numbers

    a 4×10^4 **b** 6.34×10^3 **c** 1.96×10^{-1} **d** 8.26×10^{-4}

19 Evaluate, giving each answer in standard form.

    a $(2.5 \times 10^4) \times (5 \times 10^{-2})$ **b** $(1.5 \times 10^{11}) \div (3 \times 10^{13})$

    c $(7.5 \times 10^3) + (2 \times 10^4)$ **d** $(3.4 \times 10^{-2}) - (9 \times 10^{-3})$

20 Light travels at $300\,000$ kilometres per second.

    a Write this speed in standard form.

    The star Sirius is 8.2×10^{13} km from Earth.

    b Find, to the nearest year, how long it takes light from Sirius to reach Earth.

21   Given that $a = 2$, $b = {}^-4$ and $c = \frac{1}{3}$, evaluate

    a $3a^2$ **b** $5ab$ **c** $5 - 6c$ **d** $(ab)^2$ **e** $a + b^2$ **f** $9c - b$

22   Simplify

    a $x + 5x - 2x$ **b** $4x + 8y - x + 2y$ **c** $3a - b + 3(a - 2b)$

    d $x^3 \times x^7$ **e** $x^8 \div x^9$ **f** $x^2 \times x^6 \times x^{-4}$

23   Solve each equation.

    a $2x - 3 = 17$ **b** $16 - 2x = 6$ **c** $5x + 1 = 13$

    d $7y - 2 = 4y + 7$ **e** $4(2x + 5) = 5x + 14$ **f** $3(a - 2) = 2(7 - a)$

    g $\frac{x}{3} - \frac{x}{4} = 2$ **h** $\frac{x}{6} = \frac{x-4}{3}$ **i** $\frac{3(x+1)}{4} + \frac{4x}{5} = \frac{4x-3}{2}$

24   Solve each pair of simultaneous equations

    a $x + y = 5$ **b** $2x + y = 7$ **c** $x + 2y = 17$

        $x - y = 1$ $3x + y = 13$ $3x - y = 16$

25   Make x the subject of each of the following formulae.

    a $y = 3x - 2$ **b** $y = \frac{x-4}{3}$ **c** $s = ut + \frac{1}{2}xt^2$

    d $\frac{1}{x} = \frac{1}{u} + \frac{1}{v}$ **e** $y = \frac{x+1}{x-2}$ **f** $T = 2\pi \sqrt{\frac{x}{g}}$

26   Expand

    a $(x + 3)(x + 2)$ **b** $(y + 3)(y - 1)$ **c** $(2x + 3)(x - 6)$

27   Factorise

    a $x^2 + 5x + 4$ **b** $y^2 - 5y + 6$ **c** $x^2 - 9$

    d $a^2 + 2x - 15$ **e** $x^2 - 3x - 4$ **f** $x^2 + 12x + 20$

28   A shop charges a customer £1.28 for 3 pens and 2 pencils.

    Given that a pen costs twice as much as a pencil, find the price of a pen.

29   A travel company only sells holidays for complete weeks. The cost, £C, of one of its holidays to Spain for W weeks is given by the formula

$$C = 80W + 320.$$

    a Find the cost of a 2 week holiday.

    A retired couple would like to stay in Spain for as long as possible up to a maximum cost of £1 000.

    b Calculate the longest holiday they can afford.

    c Express W in terms of C.

30 Find the gradient of the line joining the points

   a (1, 6) and (2, 8)   **b** (8, ¯2) and (¯1, 4)   **c** (¯5, ¯2) and (2, ¯8)

31 Find the gradient and y-intercept of each line.

   a $y = 2x + 7$ **b** $2y = 6x - 5$ **c** $2y + 3x - 5 = 0$

32 Find an equation of the line joining the points

   a (0, 3) and (4, 7)   **b** (1, 6) and (3, 2)   **c** (¯2, 2) and (7, 5)

33 Find the length of the line joining the points

   a (0, 5) and (3, 9)   **b** (3, ¯1) and (8, 11)   **c** (1, ¯4) and (¯3, ¯6)

34 Calculate the size of angle θ in degrees, correct to 1 dp, in each case.

   a 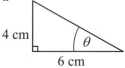   **b** 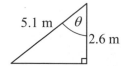   **c**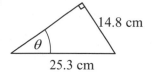

35 Calculate the length x, correct to 3 sf, in each case.

   a 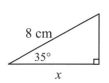   **b** 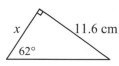   **c**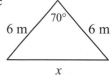

36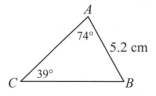

Triangle ABC is such that $\angle BAC = 74°$, $\angle ACB = 39°$ and $AB = 5.2$ cm.

   a Find the lengths of the other two sides of the triangle in cm, correct to 1 dp.

   b Calculate the area of triangle ABC in cm^2, correct to 1 dp.

37 Triangle PQR is such that $\angle PQR = 40°$, $PR = 4$ cm and $QR = 6$ cm.

Find in degrees, correct to 1 dp, the two possible values for the size of $\angle RPQ$.

38 In triangle ABC, $AB = 9$ cm, $AC = 11$ cm and $\angle CAB = 100°$.

Calculate the length BC correct to 3 sf.

39   A sphere of radius 7.6 cm is cut into 8 equal-sized pieces.

Find the volume of one piece in cm³, correct to 1 dp.

40

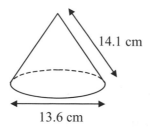

14.1 cm

13.6 cm

The slant height of a cone is 14.1 cm and the diameter of its base is 13.6 cm.

Find, correct to 3 sf,

a   the height of the cone,

b   the volume of the cone.

41

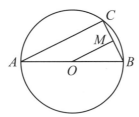

AB is a diameter of a circle, centre O.

C lies on the circle and M is the midpoint of BC

a   Write down the size of $\angle ACB$ and of $\angle CMO$.

b   Find the ratio of the area of triangle BMO to the area of trapezium $ACMO$.

42

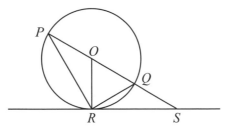

PQ is a diameter of a circle, centre O, of radius 5 cm. The tangent to the circle at R meets the projection of PQ at S.

Given that $QR = 5$ cm,

a   write down the size of $\angle ORS$ and of $\angle ORQ$,

b   find the size of $\angle ORP$ and of $\angle QPR$,

c   find the area of triangle PQR correct to 3 sf.

Indices and Surds

Exercise 2S	Skills Practice

DO NOT USE A CALCULATOR FOR THIS EXERCISE

1 Evaluate

   a $\sqrt{121}$ **b** $\sqrt[3]{64}$ **c** $\sqrt{400}$ **d** $\sqrt{\frac{1}{4}}$ **e** $\sqrt{\frac{4}{49}}$ **f** $\sqrt[4]{81}$

   g $\sqrt[3]{\frac{1}{1000}}$ **h** $\sqrt{1\frac{7}{9}}$ **i** $\sqrt{2\frac{1}{4}}$ **j** $\sqrt[3]{\frac{27}{64}}$ **k** $\sqrt{13\frac{4}{9}}$ **l** $\sqrt[3]{15\frac{5}{8}}$

2 Simplify

   a $x^2 \times x^5$ **b** $3xy \times 2x^4$ **c** $a^{\frac{1}{2}} \times a^{\frac{5}{4}}$

   d $(x^4)^2$ **e** $(b^{-2})^3$ **f** $m^7 \div m$

   g $5a^6 b \times 9a^2 b$ **h** $(8x^3 y) \div (2y^5)$ **i** $y^{\frac{4}{3}} \div y^{\frac{1}{6}}$

   j $x \times x^{\frac{3}{2}} \times x^{\frac{1}{5}}$ **k** $(5a^2 b)^4$ **l** $3x^4 \times 8x^{\frac{3}{2}}$

   m $(21p^{\frac{5}{2}}) \div (3p)$ **n** $5x^2 \times \sqrt{x}$ **o** $2x^4 \times 5x \times 3x^{-8}$

   p $(8y^5 \times x^2 y) \div (16y^3)$ **q** $(12x^{\frac{3}{2}}) \div (16x^4)$ **r** $(3ab^2)^3 \times (2a^3 b)^2$

3 Evaluate

   a 4^3 **b** $36^{\frac{1}{2}}$ **c** $27^{\frac{1}{3}}$ **d** $9^{\frac{3}{2}}$ **e** 5^0 **f** $8^{\frac{2}{3}}$

   g $4^{-\frac{1}{2}}$ **h** $\left(\frac{9}{16}\right)^{\frac{1}{2}}$ **i** $64^{-\frac{1}{3}}$ **j** $9^{-\frac{5}{2}}$ **k** $\left(\frac{1}{8}\right)^{\frac{1}{3}}$ **l** $\left(\frac{25}{81}\right)^{\frac{1}{2}}$

   m $27^{\frac{4}{3}}$ **n** $\left(\frac{4}{9}\right)^{\frac{3}{2}}$ **o** $\left(\frac{8}{27}\right)^{-\frac{1}{3}}$ **p** $\left(\frac{1}{64}\right)^{\frac{2}{3}}$ **q** $\left(1\frac{9}{16}\right)^{\frac{1}{2}}$ **r** $\left(\frac{16}{81}\right)^{-\frac{1}{4}}$

   s $32^{\frac{3}{5}}$ **t** $16^{0.75}$ **u** $(-8)^{\frac{1}{3}}$ **v** $\left(12\frac{1}{4}\right)^{-\frac{1}{2}}$ **w** $\left(2\frac{1}{4}\right)^{\frac{5}{2}}$ **x** $\left(-\frac{1}{27}\right)^{-\frac{1}{3}}$

4 Express each of the following in index notation.

   a $\sqrt{x}$ **b** $\sqrt[3]{5}$ **c** $\sqrt[5]{x}$ **d** $\left(\sqrt{10}\right)^3$ **e** $\sqrt{7^3}$ **f** $\left(\sqrt{y}\right)^3$

   g $\sqrt{a^5}$ **h** $\frac{1}{2^3}$ **i** $\frac{1}{y^4}$ **j** $\sqrt[3]{b^2}$ **k** $\sqrt[5]{b^3}$ **l** $\frac{3}{\sqrt{x}}$

5   Express each of the following in the form 2^y, where y is a function of x.

    a 4^x **b** 2×2^x **c** 8^{2x} **d** 4^{3x-1} **e** $8 \times 2^{x-1}$ **f** $8^{\frac{2}{3}x}$

6   Simplify

    a $\sqrt{12}$ **b** $\sqrt{18}$ **c** $\sqrt{50}$

    d $\sqrt{20}$ **e** $\sqrt{162}$ **f** $\sqrt{98}$

    g $\sqrt{108}$ **h** $\sqrt{1\,000}$ **i** $\sqrt{363}$

    j $\sqrt{27} + \sqrt{12}$ **k** $\sqrt{125} - \sqrt{80}$ **l** $\sqrt{75} + \sqrt{147}$

    m $5\sqrt{18} + \sqrt{8}$ **n** $4\sqrt{28} - \sqrt{63}$ **o** $\sqrt{32} + 3\sqrt{50} - \sqrt{18}$

7   Rationalise each denominator and simplify

    a $\dfrac{2}{\sqrt{2}}$ **b** $\dfrac{1}{\sqrt{3}}$ **c** $\dfrac{3}{2\sqrt{2}}$

    d $\dfrac{5}{\sqrt{45}}$ **e** $\dfrac{2\sqrt{7}}{\sqrt{21}}$ **f** $\dfrac{6\sqrt{8}}{5\sqrt{98}}$

8   Solve each equation.

    a $3^{2x-1} = 9$ **b** $16^{3x} = 4^{x+2}$ **c** $6^{x+3} = 36^x$

    d $8^{x-1} = 4^x$ **e** $64^{3x} = 16^{x-2}$ **f** $27^{\frac{x}{2}} = 9^{2x+3}$

9   Express each of the following as simply as possible with a rational denominator.

    a $\dfrac{1}{2-\sqrt{3}}$ **b** $\dfrac{3}{\sqrt{2}+1}$ **c** $\dfrac{5}{\sqrt{6}+1}$

    d $\dfrac{1}{3-\sqrt{5}}$ **e** $\dfrac{\sqrt{2}}{1+\sqrt{2}}$ **f** $\dfrac{1}{3-2\sqrt{2}}$

    g $\dfrac{4}{3+3\sqrt{5}}$ **h** $\dfrac{\sqrt{3}}{5+2\sqrt{3}}$ **i** $\dfrac{3\sqrt{7}}{4-\sqrt{7}}$

    j $\dfrac{1+\sqrt{3}}{\sqrt{3}-1}$ **k** $\dfrac{2\sqrt{2}}{3\sqrt{2}+4}$ **l** $\dfrac{\sqrt{27}+2}{3-\sqrt{3}}$

    m $\dfrac{6+\sqrt{5}}{\sqrt{5}-1}$ **n** $\dfrac{1-2\sqrt{3}}{3\sqrt{3}+4}$ **o** $\dfrac{3\sqrt{8}+1}{7-5\sqrt{2}}$

Exercise 2E   Exam Practice

1   Given that
$$a = 3^{5x} \text{ and } b = 3^{x+2},$$

  a   express each of the following in the form 3^y, where y is a function of x:

   i $3a$

   ii b^3 **(2 marks)**

  b   find the value of x for which $3a = b^3$.   **(3 marks)**

2

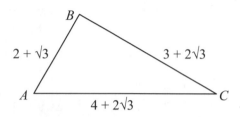

In triangle ABC, $AB = 2 + \sqrt{3}$, $AC = 4 + 2\sqrt{3}$ and $BC = 3 + 2\sqrt{3}$.

  a   Show that $\angle ABC = 90°$.   **(4 marks)**

  b   Find in its simplest form the value of $\tan(\angle BAC)$.   **(4 marks)**

3   Given that
$$25^{3x+1} = 5^{y+4}$$

  a   find an expression for y in terms of x.   **(3 marks)**

  Given also that
$$4^{3x-1} = 8^z$$

  b   show that $y = 3z$.   **(3 marks)**

4   Given that

$$\frac{x}{\sqrt{2}-1} + 7 = 4x$$

  find x in the form $a + b\sqrt{2}$ where a and b are integers.   **(5 marks)**

5   A solid right-circular cylinder has base radius of $\dfrac{1}{\sqrt{5}-2}$ cm and height of $(3\sqrt{5} + 1)$ cm.

  Show that the surface area of the cylinder can be expressed in the form $\pi(p + q\sqrt{5})$ cm^2 where p and q are integers to be found.   **(6 marks)**

Quadratics

Exercise 3S   Skills Practice

1   Factorise each of the following

    a $x^2 + 3x + 2$ **b** $x^2 + 5x + 4$ **c** $x^2 + 4x + 4$

    d $x^2 + 6x + 8$ **e** $y^2 + 13y + 36$ **f** $x^2 - 4x + 3$

    g $x^2 - 7x + 10$ **h** $x^2 - 11x + 10$ **i** $a^2 + 2a - 3$

    j $y^2 + 4y - 60$ **k** $x^2 - x - 6$ **l** $p^2 + 9p + 20$

    m $x^2 - 3x - 18$ **n** $x^2 - 9$ **o** $36 - 12a + a^2$

    p $m^2 - 49$ **q** $70 + 17x + x^2$ **r** $y^2 + y - 30$

2   Factorise to solve each of these equations.

    a $x^2 + 4x + 3 = 0$ **b** $x^2 - 2x + 1 = 0$ **c** $y^2 + 2y - 35 = 0$

    d $x^2 - 18x + 17 = 0$ **e** $12 + 7a + a^2 = 0$ **f** $45 + 4x - x^2 = 0$

    g $x^2 - 81 = 0$ **h** $m^2 + m - 56 = 0$ **i** $36 - 15x + x^2 = 0$

3   Factorise each of the following

    a $2x^2 + 3x + 1$ **b** $3y^2 - 5y - 2$ **c** $2x^2 + 11x + 12$

    d $5p^2 - 12p + 4$ **e** $1 + 7x + 6x^2$ **f** $9y^2 - 1$

    g $4x^2 - 7x + 3$ **h** $4a^2 + 4a + 1$ **i** $2 - 2x - 12x^2$

4   Factorise to solve each of these equations.

    a $5y^2 + 6y + 1 = 0$ **b** $3x^2 - 16x + 5 = 0$ **c** $3 - x - 2x^2 = 0$

    d $x^2 + 2x = 3$ **e** $3a + 4 = a^2$ **f** $x(x - 4) = 2x - 8$

    g $6 - 11m - 10m^2 = 0$ **h** $(2x - 3)^2 + 3x = 7$ **i** $9x(3 - 2x) = 10(9x + 4)$

5   Express each of the following in the form $(x + a)^2 + b$.

    a $x^2 + 2x + 3$ **b** $x^2 + 8x - 1$ **c** $x^2 - 4x + 5$

    d $x^2 + 3x + 1$ **e** $x^2 - 7x - 2$ **f** $x^2 + 16x$

    g $x^2 + x + \frac{1}{2}$ **h** $3 - 10x + x^2$ **i** $x^2 + \frac{2}{3}x + \frac{1}{6}$

6   Express each of the following in the form $a(x + b)^2 + c$.

    a $2x^2 + 4x + 1$ **b** $3x^2 - 9x - 2$ **c** $^-x^2 + 6x + 4$

    d $5x^2 + 30x - 19$ **e** $2x^2 - 3x + 5$ **f** $6x^2 + x - 1$

    g $4 - 3x - x^2$ **h** $4x^2 + 20x$ **i** $8 + 7x - 2x^2$

7 Complete the square and solve each equation. Leave answers in surd form where appropriate.

a $x^2 + 4x + 3 = 0$ **b** $y^2 - 14y + 40 = 0$ **c** $x^2 + 2x = 1$

d $18 - 10p + p^2 = 0$ **e** $2x^2 + 12x + 17 = 0$ **f** $7 + 4x - x^2 = 0$

8 Use the formula to solve each equation. Give answers correct to 2 dp where appropriate.

a $x^2 + 11x - 152 = 0$ **b** $x^2 - 2x - 3 = 0$ **c** $3x^2 + 5x + 1 = 0$

d $x(x - 3) = 5x + 4$ **e** $7m^2 + m = 3$ **f** $(3y + 1)^2 = 2 - 5y$

9 Use the formula to solve each equation. Leave answers in surd form where appropriate.

a $x^2 - 16x + 63 = 0$ **b** $3x^2 + 5x + 1 = 0$ **c** $y(3 - y) = 1$

d $12 - (2a - 5)^2 = 3a$ **e** $2x^2 - 16x + 23 = 0$ **f** $(7 - 3x)(x + 4) = 18$

10 Solve each of the following equations.

a $x + 3 - \frac{10}{x} = 0$ **b** $2y - \frac{4}{y} = 7$ **c** $x^4 - 10x^2 + 16 = 0$

d $p^{-2} + 2p^{-1} - 15 = 0$ **e** $\frac{3}{x-4} + 3 = 2x$ **f** $\frac{3x-1}{x+2} = \frac{4}{x}$

11 By evaluating the discriminant, determine for each equation whether it would have real and distinct roots, real repeated roots, or no real roots.

a $x^2 - x + 3 = 0$ **b** $x^2 + 6x + 1 = 0$ **c** $2x^2 + 2x - 5 = 0$

d $x^2 + 10x + 25 = 0$ **e** $6x^2 - 7x + 3 = 0$ **f** $16x^2 - 88x + 121 = 0$

12 For each graph find the coordinates of any points where it crosses or touches the coordinate axes. Give values correct to 2 dp where appropriate.

a $y = x^2 + 9x + 8$ **b** $y = 20 + x - x^2$ **c** $y = 2x^2 + 3x - 21$

d $y = x^2 - 4x + 5$ **e** $y = 2x^2 + 5x$ **f** $y = 5 + 7x - 2x^2$

13 Find the coordinates of the turning point of each of the following graphs. State whether the y-coordinate is a maximum or minimum value for the curve.

a $y = x^2 - 4x + 3$ **b** $y = x^2 + 2x + 7$ **c** $y = 7 + 6x - x^2$

d $y = 4x^2 + 24x + 11$ **e** $y = x^2 - 9x + 15$ **f** $y = 5 - 3x - x^2$

14 Sketch each graph. Show the coordinates of any turning points and the points of intersection with the x or y axes. Give non-exact answers correct to 2 dp.

a $y = x^2 + 6x + 8$ **b** $y = x^2 + 8x - 9$ **c** $y = x^2 - x - 6$

d $y = x^2 - 18x + 32$ **e** $y = 5 - 4x - x^2$ **f** $y = x^2 - 6x + 12$

g $y = x^2 - 3x + 1$ **h** $y = x^2 + 8x + 16$ **i** $y = 2 - 5x - x^2$

j $y = 2x^2 - 9x + 9$ **k** $y = 9x^2 - 8$ **l** $y = 7x^2 + x + 3$

Exercise 3E   Exam Practice

1   **a**   Find the values of A, B and C for which
$$2x^2 + 6x + 5 \equiv A(x + B)^2 + C.$$ **(3 marks)**

    b   Hence state the coordinates of the turning point of the curve
$$y = 2x^2 + 6x + 5.$$ **(2 marks)**

2   **a**   Express 8^{4x-2} in the form 2^y where y is a function of x.   **(1 mark)**

    b   Find the values of x for which
$$8^{4x-2} = 4^{x^2}$$

       giving your answers in the form $a + b\sqrt{6}$ where a and b are integers.   **(5 marks)**

3

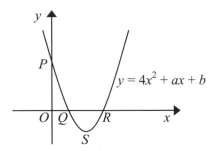

The diagram shows the curve $y = 4x^2 + ax + b$ which cuts the y-axis at the point P and the x-axis at the points Q and R.

Given that P has coordinates $(0, 33)$ and Q has coordinates $(\frac{3}{2}, 0)$

    a   calculate the values of the constants a and b,   **(3 marks)**

    b   find the coordinates of R,   **(3 marks)**

    c   find the coordinates of S, the turning point of the curve.   **(3 marks)**

4   **a**   Solve the equation
$$x + \frac{5}{x} = 6.$$ **(3 marks)**

    b   By letting $u = t^{\frac{1}{2}}$, or otherwise, find the values of t for which
$$t^{\frac{1}{2}} + 5t^{-\frac{1}{2}} = 6.$$ **(3 marks)**

5 A is the point $(2, 5)$ and B is the point $(7, k)$.

    a   Show that $AB^2 = k^2 - 10k + 50$.   **(3 marks)**

    Given also that $AB = 13$,

    b   find the possible values of k.   **(3 marks)**

6   Find the exact values of x for which

$$2(x+2) - \frac{1}{(x+3)} = x + 3.$$ **(5 marks)**

7   **a** Factorise fully the expression

$$2x^3 - 15x^2 + 18x.$$ **(2 marks)**

  b Hence, find all solutions to the equation

$$2x^3 - 15x^2 + 18x = 0.$$ **(2 marks)**

8

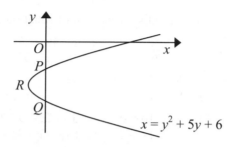

$$x = y^2 + 5y + 6$$

The diagram shows the curve $x = y^2 + 5y + 6$.

  a Find the coordinates of the points P and Q, where the curve crosses the y-axis. **(3 marks)**

  b Express the equation of the curve in the form $x = a(y + b)^2 + c$. Hence, state the coordinates of the turning point of the curve, R. **(4 marks)**

9   **a** By letting $u = x^3$, show that the equation

$$x^3(8x^3 + 7) = 1$$

can be written in the form $au^2 + bu + c = 0$. **(2 marks)**

  b By first solving your equation in u, find the values of x which satisfy the equation

$$x^3(8x^3 + 7) = 1.$$ **(3 marks)**

10   Labelling the coordinates of any points of intersection with the coordinate axes, sketch the curve $y = (x + 2)(x + k)$ when

  a $k < 0$, **(4 marks)**

  b $k = 2$. **(3 marks)**

11   **a** Given that $t = 2^x$, express each of the following in terms of t

  i 4^x
  ii 2^{x+2} **(4 marks)**

  b Using your answers to part **a**, or otherwise, solve the equation

$$4^x - 2^{x+2} - 32 = 0.$$ **(3 marks)**

Simultaneous Equations

Exercise 4S   Skills Practice

1   Find the coordinates of the point of intersection for each pair of lines.

    a $y = 2x - 3$
          b $y = \frac{1}{2}x$
          c $y = 2 - x$

       $y = x + 4$
             $y = 3x - 2$
            $y = 4x + 1$

2   Find the pair of values (x, y) which satisfy each pair of equations.

    a $2x + y = 9$
        b $4x + y = 10$
       c $x - 4y = {}^-6$

       $x - y = 3$
             $3x + y = 7$
            $2x + y = 33$

    d $2x - 3y = 29$
      e $4x - 5y = 3$
        f $4x + y = 8$

       $5x + 2y = 25$
          $3x - 8y = 15$
         $6x - 3y = {}^-15$

    g $2x + y - 14 = 0$
    h $3x + 2y - 10 = 0$
   i $3x - 2y - 9 = 0$

       $x - 3y - 21 = 0$
          $9x - 5y + 14 = 0$
        $8x + 4y - 31 = 0$

3   Find the coordinates of the points of intersection for the given curve and line.

    a $y = x^2 + 4$
        b $y = 2x - x^2$
      c $y = 5 - 2x - 4x^2$

       $y = 4x + 1$
          $y = x - 2$
          $y = 9 - 12x$

4   Solve each pair of simultaneous equations.

    a $x^2 + y - 10 = 0$
    b $y^2 + 3y - x = 4$
    c $x^2 + y^2 = 25$

       $x - y - 2 = 0$
          $2y + x = 2$
         $x - 2y = {}^-5$

    d $x^2 - y + 3 = 0$
    e $x^2 + 2xy = 15$
      f $5x^2 - y^2 = 20$

       $3x + 2y - 8 = 0$
         $x + y = 4$
          $5x - y = 10$

    g $y^2 - 2xy + 5 = 0$
    h $x^2 + 4x + y^2 = 21$
   i $2x^2 - 5xy + 18 = 0$

       $y - x + 2 = 0$
         $x + 3y = 13$
         $2x + 5y - 18 = 0$

5   Find in each case if the line and curve intersect.
    If they do so, find the coordinates of any points of intersection.

    a $x + 2y = 10$
       b $y = 2x - 5$
       c $y = x + 1$

       $x^2 + y^2 = 100$
       $y = x^2 - 2$
       $x^2 - 5y + 2y^2 = 7$

    d $x + 4y = 8$
       e $4x + 3y = 1$
      f $x - 3y = 4$

       $x^2 - xy + 2y = 14$
      $2x^2 + y - y^2 = 2$
      $2x^2 + x + y^2 = 4$

6   Solve each pair of simultaneous equations.

    a $y = \frac{2}{x} - 3$
        b $2x + \frac{1}{y} = 11$
      c $2x^2 + y^2 = 33$

       $y = x - 2$
           $x - \frac{1}{y} = 1$
          $x^2 - y^2 = 15$

Exercise 4E   Exam Practice

1   Solve the simultaneous equations

$$6x - 2xy + y^2 = 15$$
$$8x - y = 0$$

(5 marks)

2

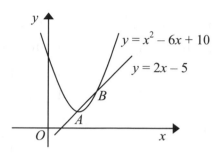

The diagram shows the curve $y = x^2 - 6x + 10$ and the line $y = 2x - 5$ which intersect at the points A and B.

a   Find the coordinates of the points A and B.   **(4 marks)**

b   Find the exact length AB in its simplest form.   **(3 marks)**

3   **a**   Given that

$$9^{2p+1} = 27^{q-2}$$

find a linear relationship between p and q.   **(2 marks)**

b   Solve the simultaneous equations

$$9^{2p+1} = 27^{q-2}$$
$$\left(\tfrac{1}{2}\right)^{q-3} = 16^{p+1}$$

(5 marks)

4   The points $(2 - a, b - 1)$ and $(3 - 2b, 5a - 9)$ lie on the line $2y - 5x + 6 = 0$.

Find the values of the constants a and b.   **(5 marks)**

5   **a**   Show that the line $y = 2x + 10$ is a tangent to the curve $y = 1 - 4x - x^2$.   **(4 marks)**

b   The line $x - y + k = 0$ is also a tangent to the curve $y = 1 - 4x - x^2$. Find the value of k.   **(4 marks)**

6   By first letting $X = \tfrac{1}{x}$ and $Y = \tfrac{1}{y}$, or otherwise, solve the simultaneous equations

$$\tfrac{3}{x} + \tfrac{2}{y} = 9$$
$$\tfrac{12}{x} - \tfrac{1}{y} = 0$$

(5 marks)

Inequalities

Exercise 5S   Skills Practice

1   Solve each inequality.

    a $3x - 1 < 14$ **b** $2b + 6 \geq 10$ **c** $2x + 3 > 4$

    d $4y + 11 \leq 3$ **e** $3x - 7 > 1$ **f** $9x - 20 < 43$

    g $3 + 2a \geq 14$ **h** $5x + 2 \leq \bar{}3$ **i** $8y - 15 > \bar{}1$

    j $13 - x < 22$ **k** $5p + 9 \geq 7$ **l** $15 - 3x \leq 11$

2   Find the set of values of x for which

    a $4x > 3x + 5$ **b** $7x - 8 \leq 3x$ **c** $5x + 1 < 4x + 9$

    d $6x \leq 4x + 5$ **e** $3(x + 2) > 9$ **f** $5x - 4 \geq 7x$

    g $5(x + 3) < 8x$ **h** $9x + 2 \leq 5x + 5$ **i** $3x + 1 > 6x + 10$

    j $x - 3 \geq \frac{1}{2}x + 1$ **k** $2(x + 4) < 3(3 - x)$ **l** $9 - 2x > x + 6$

    m $6 - 2(5 - 3x) \leq 0$ **n** $9 - 3x \geq 1 - 7x$ **o** $7(2x + 3) - 5x < 9$

3   Solve each inequality.

    a $(x - 3)(x - 5) < 0$ **b** $(x - 3)(x - 5) > 0$ **c** $(2x - 1)(x + 4) \leq 0$

    d $x^2 + 6x + 5 > 0$ **e** $a^2 + 10a + 21 \geq 0$ **f** $x^2 - 3x + 2 < 0$

    g $x^2 - 6x \geq 0$ **h** $x^2 + x - 6 \leq 0$ **i** $18 + 3y - y^2 > 0$

    j $2a^2 + 3a + 1 > 0$ **k** $5x^2 - 11x + 2 \leq 0$ **l** $b^2 + 21b + 108 < 0$

    m $3x^2 + 5x + 2 \geq 0$ **n** $y^2 + 15y - 54 < 0$ **o** $15 - 7x - 2x^2 \geq 0$

4   Solve each inequality, giving answers in surd form.

    a $x^2 - 2x - 2 < 0$ **b** $y^2 + 3y + 1 \geq 0$ **c** $x^2 - 6x + 3 > 0$

    d $4 - b - 2b^2 \leq 0$ **e** $x^2 - 8x - 4 \geq 0$ **f** $5a^2 + 7a + 1 \leq 0$

5   Giving non-exact answers correct to 2 dp, find the set of values of x for which

    a $x^2 + 9x + 20 > 0$ **b** $x^2 - 2x < 3$ **c** $x^2 - 5x + 1 \leq 0$

    d $6x^2 + 3x > 7$ **e** $2x(4x - 5) + 3 \geq 0$ **f** $x^2 < 3 - x$

    g $(x - 2)^2 > 5x - 4$ **h** $2x(3 - x) \leq x - 12$ **i** $x(7 - 2x) \geq (x + 1)^2$

6   Solve each inequality, giving non-exact answers in surd form.

    a $4x(3x - 2) \geq 0$ **b** $x^2 - 2 \leq \frac{1}{6}x$ **c** $4 - b - \frac{1}{4}b^2 > 0$

    d $20y^2 - 43y + 14 \geq 0$ **e** $\frac{1}{2}x(2 - x) < \bar{}60$ **f** $6x^2 - 8x \leq 1$

Exercise 5E   Exam Practice

1   **a**   Solve the equation

$$y(y - 3) = 10(y - 4).$$ **(3 marks)**

b   Hence, or otherwise, find the set of values of y for which

$$y(y - 3) \geq 10(y - 4).$$ **(2 marks)**

2

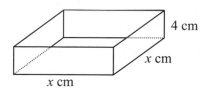

4 cm

x cm

x cm

The diagram shows an open-topped box in the shape of a cuboid of height 4 cm and with a square base of side x cm.

Given that the area of card used to make the box must be no more than 192 cm^2,

a   write down an inequality that x must satisfy.   **(3 marks)**

Given also that the volume of the box must be greater than 100 cm^3,

b   write down another inequality that x must satisfy.   **(2 marks)**

c   By solving your inequalities, find the set of possible values of x.   **(5 marks)**

3   Find the set of values of x for which

$$(2x - 1)(x - 3) < 6(x - 2).$$ **(5 marks)**

4

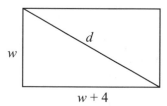

d

w

$w + 4$

The diagram shows a rectangular garden of width w metres and length $(w + 4)$ metres.

a   Show that if the length of the garden's diagonal is d metres, then

$$d^2 = 2w^2 + 8w + 16.$$ **(2 marks)**

Given also that d must be at least twice as big as w,

b   show that the maximum value of w can be expressed in the form $(a + b\sqrt{3})$ metres where a and b are integers to be found.   **(6 marks)**

Polynomials

Exercise 6S   Skills Practice

1 Giving your answers in descending powers of x, simplify

   a $(x^3 + 2x) + (x^3 + 3x^2 + 5x)$ **b** $(x^5 + 4x^4 + 2x^3) + (3x^5 + x^4 + 5x^3)$

   c $(7x^3 + x^2 + 4x) - (x^3 + 3x^2 + x)$ **d** $(x^4 + x^3 - 5x^2 + 4) + (x^3 - 3x^2 - 6)$

   e $(x^8 - 3x^6 + x^5) - (3x^7 - x^6 - 5x^5)$ **f** $(9x^3 - x^2 - 4) - (^-5x^3 + x^2 - x - 3)$

   g $(x^2 + 7x - 2 + x^{-1}) + (x - 5 + x^{-1})$ **h** $5(x^3 - 4x^2 + x) + (x^3 + 7x^2 - 3x)$

2 Giving your answers in ascending powers of x, simplify

   a $(7x + x^2 - 2x^4 - 5x^5 + x^6) + (5 - x - x^3 + x^5 + 3x^6) + (1 + 9x^2 - 6x^3 + 2x^4)$

   b $8(x^4 + 5x^3 - x^2 - 11x + 4) - 3(2x^4 - 5x^3 - x^2 + 16x + 9)$

   c $(8x^3 + x^7 - 5x - 2x^2 + x^6 - x^5) + (7x^2 - x^5 - x^4 + 12x) - (x^7 - x - x^3 - x^6)$

   d $(7x^{-2} - 2x^{-1} + 7 - x + 5x^2 - x^3) - (x^{-2} - 3x^{-1} - x + 5x^2 + x^3 - 9x^4)$

3 Giving your answers in descending powers of x, simplify

   a $(x + 2)(x^3 + 4x^2 + 8)$ **b** $(3x - 5)(2x^3 + 7x^2 + 5x - 10)$

   c $(x - 5)(1 - 2x + x^2 - 3x^3)$ **d** $(2x^2 + 3)(x^4 - 3x^3 + x + 2)$

   e $(x^2 + 3x + 1)(x^2 + x + 4)$ **f** $(x^2 - 2x + 6)(x^3 + 5x - 7)$

   g $(4x^2 + x - 3)(2x^3 - 8x^2 - x + 5)$ **h** $(2x^2 + 3 - x^{-1})(4x - 2x^{-1} + x^{-2})$

4 Find the values of the constants A and B.

   a $A(x - 3) + B(x - 4) \equiv 6x - 19$

   b $A(x + 2) + B(x - 1) \equiv 3x - 9$

   c $A(x + 2)(x + 1) + B(x + 4)(x - 1) \equiv 5x^2 + 15x - 2$

   d $A(x - 3)(x - 5) + B(2x + 1)(x - 4) \equiv 136 - 36x$

   e $A(3x - 2)(2x + 1) + Bx(4x - 6) \equiv 26x^2 - 7x - 8$

   f $A(x^2 + 5x + 3) + B(2x^2 - 3) \equiv 9x^2 + 5x - 9$

   g $A(x^2 - 3x + 2) + B(4x^2 - x + 5) \equiv 3(1 - 8x - x^2)$

   h $A(x - 1)(x^2 + 2) + B(x^3 - 5x + 1) \equiv x^3 - 5x^2 + 30x - 14$

   i $A(4x + 2 - \frac{5}{x}) + B(x - 3 + \frac{2}{x}) \equiv \frac{24}{x} - 25 - x$

   j $A(x^2 - 3)^2 + B(x - 1)^3 \equiv 4x^4 + 2x^3 - 30x^2 + 6x + 34$

   k $x(x + A)^2 + (x^2 - 4x + 2) \equiv (x - 2)^3 + B(x^2 - 10)$

5   Find the values of the constants A, B and C.

a $Ax(x-2) + B(x+1)(x+3) + C(x+3)(x-2) \equiv 6x^2 - 6x - 27$

b $A(x+3)(x-1) + B(x+2)(x-1) + C(x+2)(x-4) \equiv 4x^2 + x - 23$

c $A(x^2+1) + B(x^2-2x-3) + C(x^2+3x) \equiv 10x^2 + 7x - 11$

d $A(x+2)(x-5) + B(x+2)(x-1) + C(2x+1)(x+7) \equiv 4x^2 + 27x - 7$

e $A(x+1) + (Bx+C)(x-2) \equiv 3(x^2 - 3x - 3)$

f $A(x-5)(2x+1) + (Bx+C)(2x-1) \equiv 10x^2 - 43x - 17$

g $A(x^3 - x + 4) + (Bx+C)(x^2-1) \equiv 5x^2 - 13$

h $A(x+B)^2 + C \equiv x^2 - 4x + 1$

i $A(x+B)^2 + C \equiv 3(x+2)(x-5)$

j $Ax^6 + Bx^4 + Cx^2 \equiv x^3(5x - 3x^{-1})(x^2 + 2)$

k $Ax^4 + Bx^2 + C \equiv x^2(x - 2x^{-1})^2$

l $(x^2 + Ax)(Bx - 2) \equiv x(5x + C)(x-1)$

6   Divide

a $(x^3 + 4x^2 + 5x + 2)$ by $(x+1)$ b $(2x^3 - 11x^2 + 18x - 9)$ by $(x-3)$

c $(x^3 + 2x^2 - 7x + 6)$ by $(x-1)$ d $(x^3 + 3x^2 + 2x + 24)$ by $(x+4)$

e $(10 - 7x + 3x^2 + x^3)$ by $(x+2)$ f $(x^3 - 18x + 35)$ by $(x+5)$

g $(x^4 + x^3 - 2x^2 + 3x - 3)$ by $(x-1)$ h $(28 - 15x^2 - 5x^3 + x^4)$ by $(x-7)$

i $(4x^3 + 12x^2 - 3x - 4)$ by $(2x+1)$ j $(6x^4 - 4x^3 - 3x^2 + 5x - 1)$ by $(3x - 2)$

7   Find if $(x-2)$ is a factor of

a $x^3 - 3x - 2$ b $x^3 + 5x^2 - x + 7$ c $3x^3 - 10x^2 + 9x - 2$

8   Find if $(x+3)$ is a factor of

a $x^3 + 4x^2 + 7$ b $x^3 + 2x^2 + 3x + 18$ c $5x^3 + 17x^2 + 13x + 21$

9   Evaluate $f(^-2)$, $f(^-1)$, $f(1)$ and $f(2)$ in each case.
Hence write down any expressions that you can deduce are factors of $f(x)$.

a $f(x) \equiv x^3 + 4x^2 + 11x + 8$ b $f(x) \equiv x^3 + 5x^2 + 2x - 8$

c $f(x) \equiv 12 - 11x^2 + 2x^4$ d $f(x) \equiv 2x^4 - 4x^3 - 5x^2 + 6x + 5$

10   By first searching for a linear factor, fully factorise

a $x^3 + x^2 + 2x - 4$ b $x^3 + 2x^2 - 9x - 18$ c $x^3 + 2x^2 - 14x - 3$

d $8 + 2x - 5x^2 + x^3$ e $2x^3 - 11x^2 + 17x - 6$ f $3x^3 - 2x^2 - 37x - 12$

g $x^3 - 8$ h $1 - 5x + 5x^2 - x^3$ i $x^4 + x^3 - x - 1$

Exercise 6E   Exam Practice

1 $f(x) \equiv x^3 - 8x^2 + 17x - 10$

   a Show that $(x - 5)$ is a factor of $f(x)$.   **(2 marks)**

   b Hence, or otherwise, solve the equation $f(x) = 0$.   **(5 marks)**

2   Given that

$$(x^2 + Ax + 3)^2 \equiv x^4 + Bx^3 + Cx^2 - 12x + 9,$$

     find the values of the constants A, B and C.   **(6 marks)**

3 $f(x) \equiv 2x^3 + ax^2 + bx - 18.$

     Given that $(x + 3)$ and $(x - 2)$ are factors of $f(x)$,

   a show that $a = 5$ and $b = {}^-9$,   **(5 marks)**

   b fully factorise $f(x)$.   **(5 marks)**

4 $f(x) \equiv x^3(x + \frac{3}{x})(1 - \frac{2}{x^2})$

   a Show that $f(x)$ can be expressed in the form $(x^2 + A)(x^2 + B)$,
      where A and B are integers to be found.   **(6 marks)**

   b Hence solve the equation $f(x) = 0$.   **(3 marks)**

5

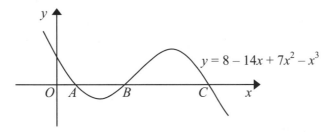

     The diagram shows the curve $y = 8 - 14x + 7x^2 - x^3$ which crosses
     the x-axis at the points A, B and C.

     Given that A is the point $(1, 0)$,

   a state one linear factor of the expression $8 - 14x + 7x^2 - x^3$,   **(1 mark)**

   b find the coordinates of the points B and C.   **(6 marks)**

6 $f(x) \equiv x^3 - x^2 + kx + 4$

     Given that $f(4) = 5f(2)$,

   a find the value of k,   **(4 marks)**

   b show that $x = {}^-1$ is a solution of the equation $f(x) = 0$,   **(1 mark)**

   c show that the equation $f(x) = 0$ has no other real solutions.   **(5 marks)**

Algebra Review

Exercise 7E   Exam Practice

1 $f(x) \equiv 2x^3 + 3x^2 - 23x - 12.$

   a   Show that $(x + 4)$ is a factor of f(x).   **(2 marks)**

   b   Find the coordinates of the points where the curve $y = $ f(x)
      intersects each of the coordinate axes.   **(6 marks)**

2   Find the set of values of x for which

$$(x - 4)^2 \geq 3(x - 1)(x - 2). \qquad \textbf{(5 marks)}$$

3

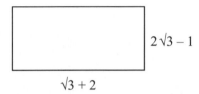

$2\sqrt{3} - 1$

$\sqrt{3} + 2$

The diagram shows a rectangle measuring $(\sqrt{3} + 2)$ cm
by $(2\sqrt{3} - 1)$ cm.

   a   Find the area of the rectangle in the form $(a + b\sqrt{3})$ cm^2.   **(2 marks)**

   b   Find the length of the diagonal of the rectangle in the
      form $p\sqrt{q}$ cm, where p and q are integers and q is prime.   **(4 marks)**

4   Solve the simultaneous equations

$$x^2 - 4x + 3y^2 - 17 = 0$$
$$2x - 3y - 4 = 0 \qquad \textbf{(6 marks)}$$

5   **a**   Express 16^{2x+1} in the form 4^y where y is a function of x.   **(2 marks)**

   b   Solve the equation

$$16^{2x+1} = 64^{x^2},$$

      giving your answers in the form $a + b\sqrt{10}$, where a and b are
      exact fractions.   **(5 marks)**

6   **a**   Find the values of A, B and C for which

$$4 - 3x - x^2 \equiv A(x + B)^2 + C. \qquad \textbf{(3 marks)}$$

   b   Sketch the curve $y = 4 - 3x - x^2$.

      Label on your sketch the coordinates of the turning point of the
      curve and the coordinates of any points where the curve meets
      the coordinate axes.   **(5 marks)**

7   The line $y = 2x - 1$ intersects the curve $y = 2 + \frac{2}{x}$ at the points A and B.

   a   Find the coordinates of the points A and B.   **(5 marks)**

   b   Find the length AB in the form $k\sqrt{5}$.   **(4 marks)**

8 $$f(x) \equiv 2x^3 + kx^2 - 7x - 10.$$

   Given that $x = {}^-2$ is a solution of the equation $f(x) = 0$,

   a   find k,   **(2 marks)**

   b   find the other solutions of the equation $f(x) = 0$, giving your answers to an appropriate degree of accuracy.   **(5 marks)**

9   Express in the form $a + b\sqrt{2}$

   a $\dfrac{6}{\sqrt{2}} + 4\sqrt{18}$ **(3 marks)**

   b $\dfrac{2 - \sqrt{2}}{3\sqrt{2} - 4}$ **(4 marks)**

10   Find the values of A, B and C for which

   a $x^2 - 5x + 7 \equiv A(x + B)^2 + C$ **(3 marks)**

   b $3x^2 + 2x - 11 \equiv (Ax + B)(x - 2) + (x + C)(x + 3)$ **(5 marks)**

11

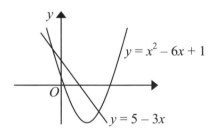

The diagram shows the line $y = 5 - 3x$ and the curve $y = x^2 - 6x + 1$.

The line and curve intersect at the points A and B.

   a   Find the coordinates of the points A and B.   **(5 marks)**

   b   Show that triangle OAB, where O is the origin, is isosceles.   **(4 marks)**

12   A cyclist accelerates for a short time before slowing down in order to find out her top speed. She moves from rest so that her speed after t seconds is $(5t - \frac{1}{2}t^2)$ metres per second.

   Find the length of time for which her speed is greater than 8 metres per second.   **(5 marks)**

13 **a** Expand $(2-3x)^3$, giving your answer in ascending powers of x.   **(3 marks)**

    b Hence, express $(2-3\sqrt{3})^3$ in the form $a+b\sqrt{3}$.   **(3 marks)**

14 **a** Solve the equation
$$x^2 - 13x + 36 = 0.$$
    (2 marks)

    b Hence, or otherwise, find the values of t for which
$$t^{\frac{4}{3}} - 13t^{\frac{2}{3}} + 36 = 0.$$
    (4 marks)

15 $$f(x) \equiv x^2 - 2\sqrt{2}\,x - 2.$$

    a Express $f(x)$ in the form $a(x + b\sqrt{2})^2 + c$.   **(4 marks)**

    b Write down the coordinates of the minimum point on the curve $y = f(x)$.   **(2 marks)**

    c Find in exact form the coordinates of the points where the curve $y = f(x)$ crosses the x-axis.   **(4 marks)**

16 $$f(x) \equiv 2x^3 + ax^2 + x + b.$$

Given that $(x + 1)$ and $(x - 4)$ are factors of $f(x)$,

    a show that $a = {}^-9$ and find the value of b,   **(5 marks)**

    b find the other linear factor of $f(x)$.   **(4 marks)**

17

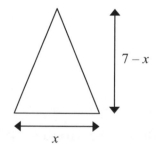

The diagram shows an isosceles triangle of base x cm and perpendicular height $(7 - x)$ cm.

    a Find the set of values of x for which the area of the triangle is greater than 3 cm^2.   **(4 marks)**

    b Find correct to 3 significant figures the value of x for which the triangle is equilateral.   **(5 marks)**

18 Solve the simultaneous equations
$$5^{2-x} = 25^y$$
$$8^x = 4^{y-3}$$
    (6 marks)

Radians, Arcs and Sectors

Exercise 8S   Skills Practice

1   Convert each angle from radians to degrees.

a $\frac{\pi}{2}$ b $\frac{\pi}{3}$ c $\frac{2\pi}{3}$ d $\frac{\pi}{12}$ e $\frac{7\pi}{6}$ f 8π

g $\frac{\pi}{9}$ h 5π i $\frac{5\pi}{4}$ j $\frac{7\pi}{3}$ k $\frac{3\pi}{8}$ l $\frac{9\pi}{2}$

2   Convert each angle from radians to degrees, correct to 1 dp.

a 1^c b 4^c c 1.6^c d 0.35^c e 8.4^c f 1.09^c

3   Convert each angle from degrees to radians, giving your answers in terms of π.

a $360°$ b $30°$ c $45°$ d $135°$ e $300°$ f $10°$

g $270°$ h $20°$ i $720°$ j $480°$ k $22.5°$ l $1350°$

4   Convert each angle from degrees to radians, correct to 2 dp.

a $50°$ b $250°$ c $34°$ d $196°$ e $18.5°$ f $710°$

Questions 5 to 8 refer to sector OAB shown below.

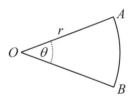

5   Calculate the length of the arc AB in cm correct to 1 dp when

a $r = 10$ cm and $\theta = \frac{\pi}{6}$ b $r = 18.5$ cm and $\theta = 45°$

6   Calculate the perimeter and the area of the sector OAB correct to 3 sf when

a $r = 5$ cm and $\theta = \frac{\pi}{3}$ b $r = 13.2$ cm and $\theta = \frac{3\pi}{4}$

c $r = 8$ cm and $\theta = 60°$ d $r = 63.5$ cm and $\theta = 102°$

7   Calculate the angle of the sector, θ, in radians correct to 2 dp when

a arc $AB = 9.2$ cm and $r = 6$ cm   b arc $AB = 28.8$ cm and $r = 7.3$ cm

8   Calculate the radius of the sector, r, in cm correct to 1 dp when

a area of sector $OAB = 23.9$ cm^2 and $\theta = \frac{\pi}{4}$

b perimeter of sector $OAB = 38.5$ cm and $\theta = 120°$

Exercise 8E   Exam Practice

1

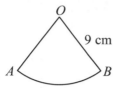

9 cm

The diagram shows the circular sector OAB, centre O, which has a radius of 9 cm and a perimeter of 22 cm.

Find

a   the length of the arc AB,   **(2 marks)**

b   the size of $\angle AOB$ in radians correct to 2 decimal places,   **(2 marks)**

c   the area of sector OAB.   **(2 marks)**

2

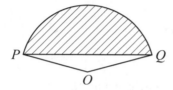

The diagram shows a circular sector OPQ of radius 12 cm in which $\angle POQ = 150°$.

Calculate

a   the area of sector OPQ, giving your answer in terms of π,   **(2 marks)**

b   the area of triangle OPQ,   **(2 marks)**

c   the area of the shaded segment in cm^2 correct to 1 decimal place.   **(2 marks)**

3

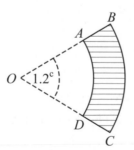

The diagram shows concentric circular sectors OAD and OBC of radius 10.6 cm and 14.2 cm respectively.

OAB and ODC are straight lines and $\angle BOC = 1.2$ radians.

Calculate correct to an appropriate level of accuracy

a   the perimeter of the shaded region,   **(4 marks)**

b   the area of the shaded region.   **(3 marks)**

4

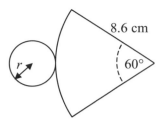

The diagram shows the net of a cone. It consists of a circular sector of radius 8.6 cm and angle 60° joined to a circle of radius r cm.

Giving your answers correct to 3 significant figures, calculate

a   the value of r,   **(4 marks)**

b   the volume of the cone.   **(5 marks)**

5

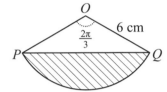

The diagram shows the sector OPQ of a circle, centre O.

Given that the radius of the circle is 6 cm and that $\angle POQ = \frac{2\pi}{3}$, find correct to 1 decimal place

a   the area of sector OPQ in cm^2,   **(2 marks)**

b   the area of the shaded segment in cm^2,   **(3 marks)**

c   the perimeter of the shaded segment in cm.   **(5 marks)**

6

A sector of a circle of radius r cm has an area of 300 cm^2.

a   Show that the angle, θ radians, subtended by the arc of the sector at its centre is given by

$$\theta = \frac{600}{r^2}.$$ **(2 marks)**

Given also that the perimeter of the sector is 72 cm,

b   show that r satisfies the equation

$$r^2 - 36r + 300 = 0,$$ **(4 marks)**

c   find the larger of the possible values of r in the form $a + b\sqrt{6}$.   **(4 marks)**

Trigonometric Ratios and Graphs

Exercise 9S   Skills Practice

1   Give the exact value of

a $\sin 30°$	**b** $\cos 30°$	**c** $\tan 45°$	**d** $\sin 120°$
e $\tan 60°$	**f** $\sin 225°$	**g** $\cos 90°$	**h** $\cos 360°$
i $\tan 390°$	**j** $\cos (^-60°)$	**k** $\sin (^-45°)$	**l** $\tan 330°$
m $\cos 240°$	**n** $\sin 690°$	**o** $\tan (^-120°)$	**p** $\sin 150°$
q $\sin (^-300°)$	**r** $\tan 720°$	**s** $\cos 585°$	**t** $\tan (^-405°)$

2   Give the exact value of

a $\cos \frac{\pi}{4}$	**b** $\tan \frac{\pi}{3}$	**c** $\sin \frac{2\pi}{3}$	**d** $\cos \frac{\pi}{6}$
e $\sin \frac{\pi}{2}$	**f** $\cos \frac{5\pi}{3}$	**g** $\tan \frac{4\pi}{3}$	**h** $\sin (^-\frac{\pi}{4})$
i $\tan (^-\frac{\pi}{6})$	**j** $\sin \frac{7\pi}{6}$	**k** $\cos (^-\frac{5\pi}{6})$	**l** $\tan 3\pi$
m $\sin \frac{7\pi}{4}$	**n** $\tan \frac{3\pi}{4}$	**o** $\cos \frac{7\pi}{2}$	**p** $\tan (^-\frac{17\pi}{6})$

In questions 3 and 4 your graphs should show the coordinates of any turning points and the equations of any asymptotes. Do not use a graphic calculator.

3   Sketch each graph in the interval $0 \le x \le 360°$.

a $y = \sin x$	**b** $y = 2\sin x$
c $y = 3\cos x$	**d** $y = \tan x$
e $y = ^-\tan x$	**f** $y = \frac{1}{4}\cos x$
g $y = \sin 2x$	**h** $y = \tan(\frac{1}{2}x)$
i $y = 2\cos 3x$	**j** $y = \sin (^-x)$
k $y = \frac{1}{2}\sin(\frac{2}{3}x)$	**l** $y = \tan(x - 90°)$
m $y = \cos(x + 30°)$	**n** $y = 4\sin(x - 45°)$
o $y = 1 + \cos x$	**p** $y = 3 - \tan x$

4   Sketch each graph in the interval $0 \le x \le 2\pi$.

a $y = \cos x$	**b** $y = \tan 2x$
c $y = \sin(x + \frac{\pi}{6})$	**d** $y = \tan(x - \frac{\pi}{4})$
e $y = ^-2\sin 3x$	**f** $y = 2 + \frac{1}{2}\cos x$
g $y = 3\tan (^-x)$	**h** $y = 3\sin(x - \frac{3\pi}{4})$

Exercise 9E   Exam Practice

1

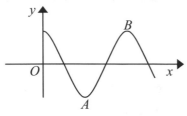

The diagram shows part of the curve $y = p \cos qx$.

The first minimum of the curve for $x > 0$ is the point A $(\frac{\pi}{3}, {}^-2)$.

a   Find the values of the constants p and q.   **(2 marks)**

b   State the period of the curve.   **(1 mark)**

c   Write down the coordinates of the point B, the first maximum
of the curve for $x > 0$.   **(2 marks)**

2   Given that

$$\tan 105° = \frac{\tan 60° + \tan 45°}{1 - (\tan 60° \times \tan 45°)}$$

a   express $\tan 105°$ in the form $a + b\sqrt{3}$,   **(5 marks)**

b   express $\tan 255°$ in the form $a + b\sqrt{3}$.   **(2 marks)**

3 $f(x) \equiv \sin x$.

Labelling clearly the coordinates of any maximum or minimum
points, sketch on separate diagrams the graphs

a $y = f(2x)$ in the interval $0 \le x \le 2\pi$,   **(4 marks)**

b $y = 1 + f(x - \frac{\pi}{6})$ in the interval $0 \le x \le 360°$.   **(4 marks)**

4   **a**

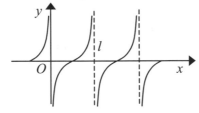

The diagram shows part of the curve $y = \tan(x + k°)$, with
x measured in degrees and $k > 0$.

i   Find the smallest possible value of the constant k.

ii   Write down the equation of the asymptote labelled l.   **(3 marks)**

b   Sketch the graph of $y = \tan({}^-2x)$ in the interval $0 \le x \le 360°$,
labelling the values of x where the graph crosses the x-axis.   **(4 marks)**

Trigonometric Equations

Exercise 10S   Skills Practice

1   Solve each equation for x in the interval $0 \leq x \leq 360°$.
    Give non-exact answers correct to 1 dp.

   a $\sin x = 0.5$ b $\sin x = 0.9$ c $\sin x = {}^-0.35$

   d $\cos x = 0.6$ e $\cos x = 0$ f $\cos x = {}^-0.146$

   g $\tan x = 0.38$ h $\tan x = {}^-1$ i $\tan x = {}^-3.675$

   j $\cos 2x = 0.5$ k $\tan 2x = 1$ l $\sin 3x = 0.219$

   m $\tan(\tfrac{1}{2}x) = 2.41$ n $\sin 2x = {}^-0.5$ o $\cos(\tfrac{1}{3}x) = {}^-0.0851$

   p $\sin(x + 30°) = 0.762$ q $\cos(x - 45°) = 0.223$ r $\tan(x + 60°) = 0.2053$

   s $\cos(x + 90°) = 0.13$ t $\tan(x - 86°) = {}^-1.24$ u $\sin(x - 204°) = {}^-0.4571$

2   Solve each equation for θ in the interval $^-180° \leq \theta \leq 180°$.
    Give non-exact answers correct to 1 dp.

   a $\tan \theta = 3.02$ b $\sin 2\theta = 0.1837$ c $\cos 3\theta = {}^-1$

   d $\cos(\theta + 90°) = 0.73$ e $\tan 4\theta = 0$ f $\sin(\theta - 34°) = {}^-0.889$

   g $2\sin \theta = 1.16$ h $2 + 5\tan \theta = 0$ i $4 - 9\cos \theta = 0$

   j $2\tan(\theta + 60°) = 9$ k $7\cos(\theta - 15°) = 4$ l $3\sin 2\theta = {}^-2.06$

3   Solve each equation for x in the interval $0 \leq x \leq 2\pi$.
    Give your answers correct to 2 dp.

   a $\tan x = 0.8$ b $\cos x = {}^-0.307$ c $\sin x = 0.955$

   d $3\cos x - 2 = 0$ e $\sin x = {}^-1$ f $\tan(x - 0.9^c) = 0.6$

   g $\sin(x + 0.25^c) = 0.71$ h $\cos(x - \tfrac{\pi}{3}) = {}^-0.68$ i $\tan(x + \tfrac{3\pi}{4}) = 1.29$

   j $\cos 2x = 0.095$ k $\tan 3x + 1 = 0$ l $\sin(\tfrac{2}{3}x) = 0.724$

4   Solve each equation for α in the interval $0 \leq \alpha \leq 2\pi$.
    Give your answers in terms of π.

   a $\sin \alpha = \tfrac{1}{2}$ b $\cos \alpha = \tfrac{\sqrt{3}}{2}$ c $\tan \alpha = 0$

   d $\cos \alpha = {}^-\tfrac{1}{2}$ e $\sin \alpha = \tfrac{1}{\sqrt{2}}$ f $\sqrt{3} - \tan \alpha = 0$

   g $\sin 2\alpha = \tfrac{\sqrt{3}}{2}$ h $\tan(\alpha - \tfrac{\pi}{6}) = 1$ i $\cos(\tfrac{1}{2}\alpha) = {}^-\tfrac{1}{\sqrt{2}}$

   j $\cos(\alpha + \tfrac{\pi}{3}) = \tfrac{1}{2}$ k $\sqrt{3}\tan 3\alpha = 1$ l $\sqrt{2} + 2\sin(\alpha - \tfrac{3\pi}{4}) = 0$

5   Solve each equation for x in the interval $0 \le x \le 360°$.
Give non-exact answers correct to 1 dp.

a $\sin(2x - 45°) = 0.5$ b $\cos(2x + 150°) = {}^-0.618$

c $\tan(3x - 20°) = 2$ d $5\sin x - 1 = 2\sin x$

e $8\cos^2 x = 4 - \cos^2 x$ f $\sin^2 x = 0.64$

g $\cos^2 2x = 0.1764$ h $(\tan x - 1)(\tan x + 3) = 0$

i $\tan^2 x + 3\tan x + 2 = 0$ j $2\cos^2 x - \cos x = 0$

k $2\sin^2 x - \sin x - 1 = 0$ l $3\tan^2 x - 5\tan x = 2$

m $\sin x(2\cos x + 1) = 0$ n $3\sin x \tan x - 2\tan x = 0$

o $4\cos^2 x + 7\cos x - 2 = 0$ p $(\tan x - 1)^2 = 2\tan x + 6$

Questions **6** and **7** refer to the diagram below.

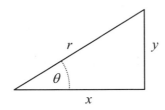

6   Write down expressions in terms of x, y and r for

a $\sin \theta$ b $\cos \theta$ c $\tan \theta$

7   Using your answers to question **6**, show that for an acute angle θ

a $\tan \theta = \dfrac{\sin \theta}{\cos \theta}$ b $\sin^2 \theta + \cos^2 \theta = 1$

8   Solve each equation for x in the interval $0 \le x \le 360°$.
Give non-exact answers correct to 1 dp.

a $\sin x = 2\cos x$ b $\cos^2 x = 4\sin^2 x$

c $2\cos^2 x - \sin x - 2 = 0$ d $5\sin^2 x - 4\cos x = 4$

e $\sin x - 3\cos x = 2\sin x$ f $2\sin^2 x - \cos^2 x = 3 - 11\sin x$

g $\sin^2 x - 5\cos^2 x = 0$ h $3\tan x = 2\cos x$

9   Solve each equation for x in the interval $^-\pi \le x \le \pi$.
Give non-exact answers correct to 2 dp.

a $\cos(2x + \frac{\pi}{6}) = 0.5$ b $\tan(\frac{1}{2}x - \frac{\pi}{4}) = 0.882$

c $\tan^2 x = 2.25$ d $3\cos^2 x = 2\cos x$

e $\sin^2 x - 4\sin x + 3 = 0$ f $5\tan^2 x = \tan x + 4$

g $2\sin x = 7\cos x$ h $3\cos^2 x - 10\sin x + 5 = 0$

i $\cos^2 x - \cos x = \sin^2 x + 2$ j $6\sin 2x \cos 2x + \sin 2x = 0$

Exercise 10E   Exam Practice

1   Find in terms of π the values of x in the interval $^-\pi \le x \le \pi$ for which

    a $\tan 2x = ^-1$,   **(4 marks)**

    b $\cos(x + \frac{\pi}{3}) = \frac{\sqrt{3}}{2}$.   **(4 marks)**

2   **a**   Sketch the curve $y = 1 + 3\sin x$ in the interval $0 \le x \le 360°$.
        Mark on your sketch the coordinates of any turning points.   **(5 marks)**

    b   Find the coordinates of the points where the curve $y = 1 + 3\sin x$
        crosses the x-axis in the interval $0 \le x \le 360°$.
        Give your answers correct to 1 decimal place.   **(4 marks)**

3   **a**   Solve for θ in the interval $^-180° \le \theta \le 180°$

        $\cos(\theta - 120°) = 0.5$.   **(4 marks)**

    b   Solve for x in the interval $0 \le x \le 360°$

        $2\cos^2 x + 3\sin x = 3$.   **(5 marks)**

4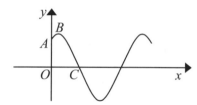

The diagram shows part of the curve $y = \cos(2x - 30°)$ with
x measured in degrees.

Find the exact coordinates of

    a   the point A, where the curve meets the y-axis,   **(2 marks)**

    b   the point B, the first maximum on the curve for $x > 0$,   **(3 marks)**

    c   the point C, where the curve first crosses the x-axis for $x > 0$,   **(3 marks)**

5   Find in terms of π the values of θ in the interval $0 \le \theta \le 2\pi$ for which

    a $\sin^2 \theta = \frac{3}{4}$,   **(5 marks)**

    b $\sin \theta - \cos \theta = 0$.   **(4 marks)**

6   The curve $y = k\sin(x - 60°)$, with x measured in degrees passes
through the point $(105, 2\sqrt{2})$.

    a   Find the value of k.   **(3 marks)**

    b   Sketch the curve for x in the interval $0 \le x \le 360°$.
        Label on your sketch the coordinates of the points where the
        curve intersects the coordinate axes.   **(5 marks)**

Trigonometry Review

Exercise 11E	Exam Practice

1 Find the values of θ in the interval $0 \le \theta \le 360°$ for which

    a $\sin(\theta - 15°) = \dfrac{1}{\sqrt{2}}$ **(4 marks)**

    b $4\cos^2\theta = 1$ **(5 marks)**

2

The diagram shows a circular sector OPQ.

Given that $OP = 9.5$ cm and that the area of the sector is 64 cm^2, find correct to 3 significant figures

    a the size of $\angle POQ$ in radians,   **(3 marks)**

    b the area of the shaded segment in cm^2.   **(3 marks)**

3   **a** Solve the equation

$$2x^2 - x = 2$$

    giving your answers correct to 4 significant figures.   **(4 marks)**

    b Hence, find correct to an appropriate level of accuracy, the values of θ in the interval $^-\pi \le \theta \le \pi$ for which

$$2\sin^2\theta - \sin\theta = 2.$$

                                                     (4 marks)

4

The diagram shows the sector of a circle of radius r cm

Given that the perimeter of the sector is 30 cm,

    a show that the area of the sector is given by $(15r - r^2)$ cm^2,   **(4 marks)**

    b find the set of values of r for which the area of the sector is more than 50 cm^2.   **(4 marks)**

5   **a** Sketch the curve $y = \tan 2x$ for x in the interval $0 \le x \le 360°$.   **(3 marks)**

    b Find the values of θ in the interval $^-180° \le \theta \le 180°$ for which

$$3\sin^2\theta - \cos^2\theta = 2\cos\theta + 3.$$

                                                     (6 marks)

6

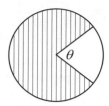

The diagram shows a circle divided into a minor sector of angle θ radians and a major sector, which is shaded.

Given that the perimeter of the major sector is twice the perimeter of the minor sector

a find θ in terms of π,   **(4 marks)**

b show that the ratio of the area of the major sector to the area of the minor sector is

$$2\pi + 1 : \pi - 1$$ **(4 marks)**

7 $$f(x) \equiv \sin\left(2x + \frac{\pi}{4}\right)$$

a State the value of f(0).   **(1 mark)**

b Solve the equation $f(x) = 0$ for x in the interval $0 \le x \le 2\pi$ giving your answers in terms of π.   **(5 marks)**

c Sketch the curve $y = f(x)$ in the interval $0 \le x \le 2\pi$.   **(3 marks)**

8 **a** Solve the equation

$$4y + 6y^{-1} = 11.$$ **(4 marks)**

b Hence, find correct to 1 decimal place the values of x in the interval $0 \le x \le 360°$ for which

$$4\tan x + \frac{6}{\tan x} = 11.$$ **(4 marks)**

9

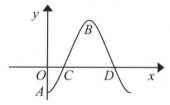

The diagram shows part of the curve $y = 1 - 3\cos x$ for x in the interval $0 \le x \le 360°$.

a State the coordinates of the point A, where the curve meets the y-axis.   **(1 mark)**

b State the coordinates of the point B, the maximum on the curve.   **(2 marks)**

c Find the x-coordinates of the points C and D, where the curve meets the x-axis, giving your answers correct to 1 decimal place.   **(4 marks)**

10   Given that $\sin 75° = \frac{1}{4}(\sqrt{6} + \sqrt{2})$ and $\cos 75° = \frac{1}{4}(\sqrt{6} - \sqrt{2})$,

find $\tan 75°$ in the form $a + b\sqrt{3}$.   **(5 marks)**

11   The curve $y = a\cos bx$ with x measured in degrees passes through
the points $(0, 4)$ and $(135, 2\sqrt{2})$.

a   Find the value of the constant a.   **(2 marks)**

Given that $0 \le b \le 1$,

b   find the value of the constant b,   **(4 marks)**

c   sketch the curve for x in the interval $0 \le x \le 360°$.   **(3 marks)**

12

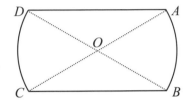

The diagram shows the shape of a tray. It consists of two identical
circular sectors OAB and OCD and two triangles OAD and OBC.

Given that $\angle AOB = 60°$ and $OA = 24$ cm,

a   show that the perimeter of the tray is $16(\pi + 3\sqrt{3})$ cm,   **(5 marks)**

b   find the area of the tray in exact form.   **(5 marks)**

13 $f(x) \equiv (\sin x - \cos x)^2 + \sin x - 1.$

a   Show that $f(x)$ can also be written as

$$f(x) \equiv \sin x(1 - 2\cos x).$$ **(3 marks)**

b   Hence, or otherwise, solve the equation $f(x) = 0$ for x in the
interval $0 \le x \le 2\pi$ giving your answers in terms of π.   **(5 marks)**

14

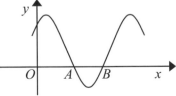

The diagram shows part of the curve $y = 1 + 2\sin(3x + k)$ where
x is measured in degrees and $0 \le k \le 90°$.

a   State the period of the curve.   **(1 mark)**

Given that the curve passes through the point $(20, 3)$,

b   show that $k = 30$,   **(3 marks)**

c   find the coordinates of the points A and B, the first two points
where the curve crosses the x-axis for $x > 0$.   **(6 marks)**

Arithmetic Series

Exercise 12S   Skills Practice

1   Write down the first 5 terms of sequences whose nth term, u_n, is given by

    a $u_n = 3n + 1$ **b** $u_n = 6n - 5$ **c** $u_n = 11n - 28$

    d $u_n = 25 - 4n$ **e** $u_n = 1.5n + 3.5$ **f** $u_n = 5 - 15n$

2   Find an expression for the nth term of sequences beginning

    a 7, 9, 11, 13, ...   **b** 2, 6, 10, 14, ...   **c** 35, 28, 21, 14, ...

    d $^-$12, $^-$7, $^-$2, 3, ...   **e** 17, 4, $^-$9, $^-$22, ...   **f** 0.4, 1.2, 2.0, 2.8, ...

3   Write down the 10th and 25th terms of each of the sequences in question **2**.

4   The sum of the first n terms of a series, S_n, is given by $S_n = 3n^2$.

    a Evaluate S_2 and S_3.

    b Hence, find the 3rd term of the series

    c Find an expression for S_{n-1}, the sum of the first $(n-1)$ terms of the sequence.

    d Hence, find an expression for the nth term of the sequence.

5   The sum of the first n terms of a series, S_n, is given by $S_n = 25n - 6n^2$.

    Find an expression for the nth term of the series.

6   Use a suitable formula to find the sum of each series.

    a $5 + 11 + 17 + 23 + 29 + 35 + 41 + 47 + 53 + 59$

    b $22 + 19 + 16 + 13 + 10 + 7 + 4 + 1 + (^-2) + (^-5) + (^-8)$

7   The first term, a, the common difference, d, and the number of terms, n, is given for each of three series. Find the sum of each series.

    a $a = 5$; $d = 2$; $n = 10$.

    b $a = 17$; $d = 6$; $n = 45$.

    c $a = 50$; $d = ^-4$; $n = 14$.

8   The first term, a, the common difference, d, and the last term, l, is given for each of three series. Find the number of terms in each series.

    a $a = 3$; $d = 7$; $l = 241$.

    b $a = ^-8$; $d = 9$; $l = 46$.

    c $a = 387$; $d = ^-11$; $l = 35$.

9   Find the sum of each series in question **8**.

10   Evaluate

   a $\displaystyle\sum_{r=1}^{6}(2r+1)$ **b** $\displaystyle\sum_{r=1}^{15}(8r-3)$ **c** $\displaystyle\sum_{r=1}^{34}(3r+9)$

   d $\displaystyle\sum_{r=1}^{11}(35-r)$ **e** $\displaystyle\sum_{r=3}^{18}(7r+20)$ **f** $\displaystyle\sum_{r=8}^{40}(14-2r)$

11   An arithmetic series begins $2\frac{1}{2}+4\frac{1}{4}+6+7\frac{3}{4}+9\frac{1}{2}+...$.

   a Find an expression for the nth term of the series.

   b Find the sum of the first 20 terms of the series.

12   **a** Find the sum of the series $1+2+3+4+...+100$.

   b Find the sum of the series $5+10+15+20+...+100$.

   c Find the sum of the integers, between 1 and 100 inclusive, not divisible by 5.

13   Find the sum of the integers, between 1 and 300 inclusive, not divisible by 3.

14   The first and 5th terms of an arithmetic series are 4 and 16 respectively.

   a Find the common difference of the series.

   b Find the sum of the first 10 terms of the series.

15   The second and third terms of an arithmetic series are 26.5 and 31 respectively.

   a Find the first term and common difference of the series.

   b Given that the last term is 445, find the number of terms in the series.

16   The 4th and 7th terms of an arithmetic series are 7 and ⁻5 respectively.

   a Find the first term and common difference of the series.

   b Find an expression in terms of n for the sum of the first n terms of the series.

17   The third term of an arithmetic series is 18. The sum of the first six terms of the series is 132.

   a Find the first term and common difference of the series.

   b Find the sum of the first 26 terms of the series.

18   The 4th term of an arithmetic series is 23. The sum of the first eight terms of the series is 214.

   a Find the first term and common difference of the series.

   b Find the least value of n for which the sum of the first n terms of the series is greater than 1000.

Exercise 12E	Exam Practice

1 The third and fifth terms of an arithmetic series are ¯3 and 5 respectively.

    a Find the first term and common difference the of the series. **(4 marks)**

    b Find the sum of the first 50 terms of the series. **(2 marks)**

2 Natasha decides to go swimming on three evenings each week.

    In the first week she swims 8 lengths on each visit to the pool. In each subsequent week she increases by two the number of lengths that she swims on each of her visits to the pool during that week.

    a Show that in the first three weeks she swims 90 lengths in total. **(2 marks)**

    b In the nth week of her visits the total number of lengths that she has completed passes 2000. Find the value of n. **(5 marks)**

3   **a** The sixth term of an arithmetic series is 38.

      Given that the common difference of the series is k, find expressions in terms of k for

      i the first term of the series,

      ii the sum of the first 20 terms of the series. **(5 marks)**

    b Evaluate $\displaystyle\sum_{r=1}^{18}(16-\tfrac{3}{2}r)$. **(4 marks)**

4 The first three terms of an arithmetic series are $(4x-5)$, $3x$ and $(x+13)$ respectively.

    a Find the value of x. **(3 marks)**

    b Given that the sum of the first n terms of the series is 126, find the two possible values of n. **(5 marks)**

5 The sum of the first four terms of an arithmetic series is 96.

    The sum of the fifth, sixth and seventh terms of the series is 219.

    a Find the first term and common difference of the series. **(6 marks)**

    b Find and simplify an expression in terms of n for the sum of the first n terms of the series. **(4 marks)**

6   **a** Evaluate $\displaystyle\sum_{r=8}^{32}7r-11$. **(4 marks)**

    b The rth term of an arithmetic series is given by $(3r+5)$.

      Given that the sum of the first n terms is 665, find the value of n. **(6 marks)**

Geometric Series

Exercise 13S   Skills Practice

1   Write down the first 4 terms of sequences whose nth term, u_n, is given by

    a $u_n = 3^n$ **b** $u_n = 7^n$ **c** $u_n = (^-4)^n$

    d $u_n = 3 \times 2^n$ **e** $u_n = 6^{n-1}$ **f** $u_n = (\frac{2}{3})^n$

2   Find an expression for the nth term of sequences beginning

    a   5, 25, 125, 625, ...   **b** $\frac{1}{2}$, $\frac{1}{4}$, $\frac{1}{8}$, $\frac{1}{16}$, ...   **c**   12, 36, 108, 324, ...

    d $^-2$, 4, $^-8$, 16, ...   **e**   12, 4, $\frac{4}{3}$, $\frac{4}{9}$, ...   **f** $\frac{1}{2}$, 1, 2, 4, ...

3   Use the formula to find the sum of each series.

    a $5 + 10 + 20 + 40 + 80 + 160 + 320 + 640$

    b $(^-3) + 9 + (^-27) + 81 + (^-243) + 729 + (^-2187)$

    c $96 + 48 + 24 + 12 + 6 + 3 + \frac{3}{2} + \frac{3}{4} + \frac{3}{8} + \frac{3}{16}$

4   The sum of the first n terms of a geometric series, S_n, is given by $S_n = (2^{n+1} - 2)$.

    a   Evaluate S_1, S_2 and S_3.

    b   Find the first three terms of the series.

    c   Find the 6th term of the series.

5   The sum of the first n terms of a geometric series, S_n, is given by $S_n = 4(3^n - 1)$.

    Find the 5th term of the series.

6   The first term, a, the common ratio, r, and the number of terms, n, are given for each of three series.

    Find the sum of each series giving non-exact answers correct to 2 dp.

    a $a = 5;$ $r = 2;$ $n = 10.$

    b $a = 180;$ $r = \frac{1}{3};$ $n = 8.$

    c $a = 0.16;$ $r = ^-2.5;$ $n = 12.$

7   The first term, a, and the common ratio, r, are given for each of three series.
Find the sum to infinity of each series giving non-exact answers correct to 2 dp.

    a $a = 10;$ $r = \frac{1}{2}.$

    b $a = 360;$ $r = 0.85.$

    c $a = 92;$ $r = ^-\frac{3}{4}.$

8 Evaluate correct to 4 sf

a $\displaystyle\sum_{r=1}^{16} 2^r$ **b** $\displaystyle\sum_{r=1}^{10} (4 \times 3^r)$ **c** $\displaystyle\sum_{r=1}^{8} (\tfrac{1}{2})^r$

d $\displaystyle\sum_{r=1}^{8} 5^{n-2}$ **e** $\displaystyle\sum_{r=3}^{10} 3^r$ **f** $\displaystyle\sum_{r=6}^{12} \left[80 \times (\tfrac{4}{5})^r\right]$

9 A geometric series begins $2 + 3 + 4.5 + 6.75 + 10.125 + \ldots$.

  a Find an expression for the nth term of the series.

  b Explain why you cannot calculate the sum to infinity of this series.

10 The first term of a geometric series is 15 and its sum to infinity is 40.

  a Find the common ratio of the series.

  b Find the sum of the first six terms of the series correct to 2 dp.

11 The first term of a geometric series is 252 and its sum to infinity is 216.

  a Find the common ratio of the series.

  b Find as an exact fraction the 5th term of the series.

12 The first and 4th terms of a geometric series are 80 and 10 respectively.

  a Find the common ratio of the series.

  b Find the sum to infinity of the series.

13 The second and 5th terms of a geometric series are $^-15$ and 405 respectively.

  a Find the first term and common ratio of the series.

  b Find the sum of the first nine terms of the series.

14 There are estimated to be 20 000 fish in a lake.
It is assumed that this number will increase by 10% each year.

  a How many fish will there be in the lake after one year?

  b How many fish will there be in the lake after three years?

  c By what percentage will the number of fish in the lake increase in four years?

15 £5000 is invested in an account giving 6% per annum compound interest.

  a How much will be in the account after three years?

  b How much interest will have been paid into the account after eight years?

16 The second term of a geometric series is 36.
The sum of the first two terms of the series is $^-18$.

  a Find the first term and common ratio of the series.

  b Find the sum to infinity of the series.

Exercise 13E	Exam Practice

1   The second and fourth terms of a geometric series are 108 and 3 respectively.

    a   Find the two possible values of the common ratio of the series.   **(3 marks)**

    b   Find the sum to infinity corresponding to each of your values for the common ratio. Give your answers correct to 1 decimal place.   **(5 marks)**

2   £2000 is paid into an account at the start of each year.

    The account pays 5% per annum compound interest.

    a   Find the amount in the account at the end of the second year.   **(2 marks)**

    b   Show that the amount in the account at the end of n years is given by $k[(1.05)^n - 1]$ and find the value of the constant k.   **(5 marks)**

3   The first term and common ratio of a geometric series are $\dfrac{1}{2 - \sqrt{3}}$

    and $(\sqrt{3} - 1)$ respectively.

    Find in the form $a + b\sqrt{3}$

    a   the second term of the series,   **(4 marks)**

    b   the sum to infinity of the series.   **(4 marks)**

4   The first three terms of a geometric series are $(3p + 1)$, $(2p - 1)$ and $(p + 1)$ respectively, where p is a non-zero constant.

    a   Find the value of p.   **(5 marks)**

    b   Find the sum to infinity of the series.   **(4 marks)**

5   A ball is projected vertically upwards from ground level reaching a greatest height of 12 m above the ground. It falls to the ground and bounces up and down vertically.

    Given that after each bounce the greatest height then reached by the ball is reduced by 25%,

    a   show that after the second bounce it reaches a height of 6.75 m,   **(2 marks)**

    b   find, correct to 3 significant figures, the total distance that the ball has travelled when it hits the ground for the 10th time.   **(5 marks)**

6   The third and sixth terms of a geometric series are 8 and k^3 respectively, where k is a constant.

    a   Find the common ratio of the series in terms of k.   **(3 marks)**

    b   Find the first term of the series in terms of k.   **(2 marks)**

    c   Given that $k = {}^-4$, find the sum of the first nine terms of the series.   **(4 marks)**

Sequences and Series Review

Exercise 14E   Exam Practice

1   The fourth term of an arithmetic series is 3.

The sum of the first six terms of the series is 6.

   a Find the first term and the common difference of the series.   **(5 marks)**

   b Find the sum of the first 60 terms of the series.   **(3 marks)**

2   The third and fourth terms of a geometric series are 24 and 16 respectively.

   a Find the first term and the common ratio of the series.   **(4 marks)**

   b Find the sum to infinity of the series.   **(2 marks)**

3   In its business plan, a company predicts that it will make £26 000 profit in the year 2001. The plan predicts that in subsequent years the company's profits will increase by £3500 each year.

   a Show that the plan predicts a profit of £33 000 in the year 2003.   **(2 marks)**

   b By summing an appropriate series, find the total profit that the company will make, according to the business plan, in the years 2001 to 2012 inclusive.   **(4 marks)**

4   The first term and common difference of an arithmetic series are 79 and $^-4$ respectively.

   a Find and simplify an expression for the nth term of the series.   **(2 marks)**

   b By forming a suitable inequality and solving it, find out how many terms of the series are positive.   **(3 marks)**

   c Hence, or otherwise, find the greatest value of S_n, the sum of the first n terms of the series.   **(4 marks)**

5   The first and third terms of a geometric series are 12 and 4 respectively.

Given that the common ratio is positive,

   a find the common ratio of the series in the form $k\sqrt{3}$, where k is an exact fraction,   **(4 marks)**

   b find the ninth term of the series as an exact fraction,   **(3 marks)**

   c show that the sum to infinity of the series is $6(3 + \sqrt{3})$.   **(4 marks)**

6   The sum to infinity of a geometric series is equal to three times the first term.

    a   Find the common ratio of the series.   **(3 marks)**

    Given that the sum of the first k terms of the series is equal to twice the first term,

    b   show that $(\frac{2}{3})^k = \frac{1}{3}$.   **(4 marks)**

7   The first and third terms of an arithmetic series are 6 and $4x$ respectively.

    Find and simplify expressions in terms of x for

    a   the common difference of the series,   **(3 marks)**

    b   the fifth term of the series,   **(3 marks)**

    c   the sum of the first eight terms of the series.   **(3 marks)**

8   **a**   Evaluate correct to 4 significant figures

$$\sum_{r=1}^{10} (\tfrac{4}{3})^r .$$

                                                                                (4 marks)

    b   Find the sum of the even numbers between 101 and 199.   **(5 marks)**

9   The nth term of a sequence, u_n, is given by

$$u_n = k^n + n.$$

    Given that $u_4 = 2u_2$ and that $k > 0$,

    a   show that $k = \sqrt{2}$,   **(4 marks)**

    b   find $\dfrac{u_6}{u_5}$ in the form $a + b\sqrt{2}$.   **(5 marks)**

10   The first term of an arithmetic series is 75.

    The sum of the first ten terms of the series is 480.

    a   Find the common difference of the series.   **(4 marks)**

    b   Find the other value of n for which the sum of the first n terms of the series is 480.   **(5 marks)**

11   A savings account pays 0.8% interest on the amount in the account at the end of each month.

    a   Brian invests £1000 in this account.

        Show that after the payment of interest at the end of the first year there is £1100.34 in his account, to the nearest penny.   **(3 marks)**

    b   Tahira pays £200 into this account at the start of each month.

        Find to the nearest penny the amount in her account after the payment of interest at the end of a two year period.   **(6 marks)**

Coordinate Geometry

Exercise 15S   Skills Practice

1   Write down in the form $(y - y_1) = m(x - x_1)$ the equation of a line passing through the given point and with the given gradient, m.

   a $(4, 3)$; $m = 2$ **b** $(5, 0)$; $m = \frac{1}{2}$ **c** $(^-1, 6)$; $m = 3$

   d $(^-5, 5)$; $m = 1$ **e** $(8, \frac{5}{2})$; $m = ^-4$ **f** $(^-7, ^-2)$; $m = \frac{3}{4}$

2   Find in the form $y = mx + c$ the equation of a line passing through the given point and with the given gradient, m.

   a $(0, 6)$; $m = 3$ **b** $(3, 3)$; $m = 1$ **c** $(4, 9)$; $m = ^-2$

   d $(^-6, 8)$; $m = \frac{1}{3}$ **e** $(\frac{3}{2}, 4)$; $m = 5$ **f** $(^-8, 0)$; $m = ^-\frac{1}{2}$

3   Find in the form $ax + by + c = 0$ the equation of a line passing through the given point and with the given gradient, m.

   a $(4, 0)$; $m = 1$ **b** $(18, 6)$; $m = ^-2$ **c** $(^-4, 4)$; $m = ^-1$

   d $(5, 2)$; $m = 3$ **e** $(4, \frac{7}{2})$; $m = \frac{1}{4}$ **f** $(^-9, ^-6)$; $m = ^-\frac{3}{5}$

4   Find in the form $y = mx + c$ the equation of a line passing through the points

   a $(2, 6)$ and $(4, 8)$ **b** $(^-10, 0)$ and $(0, 5)$ **c** $(3, 1)$ and $(7, 9)$

   d $(^-6, ^-2)$ and $(3, 4)$ **e** $(0, 8)$ and $(5, ^-2)$ **f** $(\frac{3}{4}, ^-1)$ and $(2, ^-\frac{5}{4})$

5   Find in the form $ax + by + c = 0$ the equation of a line passing through the points

   a $(9, 1)$ and $(13, 5)$ **b** $(^-2, 0)$ and $(0, ^-2)$ **c** $(^-1, 2)$ and $(5, 6)$

   d $(7, \frac{1}{2})$ and $(11, 1)$ **e** $(^-4, ^-6)$ and $(2, 9)$ **f** $(^-6, \frac{3}{5})$ and $(1, ^-5)$

6   Find the gradient of each line.

   a $y = x + 3$ **b** $y = 2 - 3x$ **c** $5x - y + 2 = 0$

   d $3x + y - 4 = 0$ **e** $x - 2y - 7 = 0$ **f** $x + y = 0$

   g $7x - 2y = 4$ **h** $2x + 10y - 11 = 0$ **i** $8x + 5y - 19 = 0$

7   State any pairs of lines in question **6** that are parallel.

8   State any pairs of lines in question **6** that are perpendicular.

9   Find the equation of a line passing through the given point and parallel to the given line. Give your equation in the form $y = mx + c$.

   a $(1, 2)$; $y = 3x - 4$ **b** $(4, 0)$; $y = 6 - x$

   c $(3, 8)$; $2x - 3y + 4 = 0$ **d** $(^-7, 5)$; $x + 4y = 5$

10   Find the equation of a line passing through the given point and perpendicular to the given line. Give your equation in the form $ax + by + c = 0$.

   a $(9, 1)$; $y = 2x - 4$ **b** $(^-3, ^-2)$; $y = ^-3x + 7$

   c $(5, 4)$; $3x - 2y = 0$ **d** $(6, ^-3)$; $5x + 4y + 8 = 0$

11   Find the coordinates of the mid-point of a line joining each pair of points.

   a $(0, 0)$ and $(8, 4)$ **b** $(2, 6)$ and $(10, 4)$ **c** $(1, 3)$ and $(4, 17)$

   d $(^-4, 12)$ and $(0, 2)$ **e** $(^-7, ^-3)$ and $(4, 4)$ **f** $(\frac{3}{2}, 6)$ and $(7, ^-7)$

12   Find the equation of the perpendicular bisector of a line joining each pair of points. Give your equation in the form $ax + by + c = 0$.

   a $(2, 0)$ and $(4, 2)$ **b** $(^-4, 1)$ and $(4, 5)$ **c** $(1, 1)$ and $(3, 5)$

   d $(0, 8)$ and $(4, 2)$ **e** $(^-6, 1)$ and $(2, 7)$ **f** $(^-1, ^-1)$ and $(4, 5)$

13   A line has gradient 2 and passes through the point $(1, 8)$.

   a   Find the equation of the line in the form $y = mx + c$.

   b   Find the coordinates of the points where the line intersects the coordinate axes.

14   The line l_1 passes through the points A $(1, 9)$ and B $(4, ^-3)$.

   a   Find the equation of the line l_1 in the form $y = mx + c$.

   The line l_2 is parallel to the line l_1 and passes through the point C $(^-5, ^-1)$

   b   Find the equation of the line l_2 in the form $y = mx + c$.

15   The line l passes through the points A $(^-8, 0)$ and B $(0, 4)$.

   a   Find the equation of the line l in the form $ax + by + c = 0$.

   b   Find the coordinates of the point C, the mid-point of AB.

   c   Find in surd form the length OC where O is the origin.

16   The line l has a gradient of $^-2$ and passes through the point A $(3, 4)$.

   a   Find an equation of the line l.

   b   Find the coordinates of the points B and C where the line intersects the coordinate axes.

   c   Find the area of triangle OBC where O is the origin.

17   The line l passes through the points P $(^-2, 3)$ and Q $(4, 7)$.

   a   Find the equation of the line l in the form $ax + by + c = 0$.

   The line m is perpendicular to the line l and passes through the point R $(3, 2)$.

   b   Find an equation of the line m.

   c   Find the coordinates of the point S where l and m intersect.

Exercise 15E	Exam Practice

1   The line l_1 has gradient $\frac{2}{3}$ and passes through the point A (1, 4).

    a Find the equation of the line l_1 in the form $ax + by + c = 0$.   **(2 marks)**

    The line l_2 passes through the points B (6, 0) and C (8, 4).

    b Find an equation of the line l_2.   **(3 marks)**

    The line l_3 is perpendicular to l_1 and passes through the point A. The lines l_2 and l_3 intersect at the point D.

    c Find the coordinates of the point D.   **(5 marks)**

2   The line l has equation $2x + 8y = 17$ and intersects the x-axis at the point A.

    a Find the coordinates of the point A.   **(2 marks)**

    The line m passes through the origin O and is perpendicular to the line l. The lines l and m intersect at the point B.

    b Find the coordinates of the point B.   **(5 marks)**

    c Find the area of triangle OAB.   **(3 marks)**

3   The line l passes through the points A (3, 16) and B (11, 12).

    a Find the equation of the line l in the form $ax + by + c = 0$.   **(3 marks)**

    b Find the coordinates of the point C, the mid-point of AB.   **(2 marks)**

    c Show that the perpendicular bisector of AB passes through the origin.   **(4 marks)**

4   The line l passes through the points A ($^-2$, 3) and B (6, 9).

    a Find the equation of the line l in the form $ax + by + c = 0$.   **(3 marks)**

    The line l intersects the coordinate axes at the points C and D.

    b Find the perimeter of triangle OCD, where O is the origin.   **(6 marks)**

5   The line l_1 has a gradient of 3 and passes through the point A (1, 12).

    a Find the equation of the line l_1 in the form $y = mx + c$.   **(2 marks)**

    The line l_2 is parallel to l_1 and intersects the y-axis at the point A $(0, \frac{21}{2})$.

    b Find an equation of the line l_2 in the form $ax + by + c = 0$.   **(2 marks)**

    c Show that the area of the trapezium bounded by the lines l_1, l_2 and the coordinate axes is $\frac{39}{8}$.   **(6 marks)**

Differentiation

Exercise 16S   Skills Practice

1   Differentiate with respect to x.

   a x^2 **b** x^7 **c** x^4 **d** x^{-2} **e** x^{-5} **f** x

   g 7 **h** $5x$ **i** $4x^2$ **j** $2x^3$ **k** $6x^{-4}$ **l** $8x^{-3}$

2   Differentiate with respect to t.

   a t^3 **b** $10t$ **c** $2t^{-1}$ **d** 8 **e** $t^{\frac{1}{2}}$ **f** $4t^{\frac{5}{2}}$

   g $6t^{-\frac{1}{2}}$ **h** $3t^{\frac{3}{2}}$ **i** $9t^{\frac{2}{3}}$ **j** $5t^{-\frac{3}{4}}$ **k** $\frac{1}{2}t^{\frac{4}{3}}$ **l** $\frac{5}{3}t^{\frac{6}{5}}$

3   Find $f'(x)$

   a $f(x) \equiv x^3 + 5x^2$ **b** $f(x) \equiv 2x^4 - 3x$ **c** $f(x) \equiv 8x + 4x^{-3}$

   d $f(x) \equiv x^7 + 6x^5 - x^3$ **e** $f(x) \equiv x(x^2 - 3)$ **f** $f(x) \equiv (x + 1)(x - 5)$

   g $f(x) \equiv (x + 7)(3x - 1)$ **h** $f(x) \equiv (2x + 1)(x - 9)$ **i** $f(x) \equiv 9x + 4x^{\frac{1}{2}}$

   j $f(x) \equiv 6x^{\frac{5}{2}} - x^{-1}$ **k** $f(x) \equiv 6x^{\frac{4}{3}} - 2x^{\frac{1}{3}}$ **l** $f(x) \equiv \frac{1}{2}x^{-2} + \frac{2}{3}x^{-\frac{7}{2}}$

4   Differentiate with respect to x.

   a $\frac{3}{x}$ **b** $\frac{1}{3x}$ **c** $\sqrt{x}$ **d** $\frac{6}{\sqrt{x}}$ **e** $\sqrt[3]{x}$ **f** $\sqrt{x^3}$

5   Find $\frac{dy}{dx}$ in each case

   a $y = 18x^2 - x + 2$ **b** $y = x^3 + 4x + 3x^{-2}$ **c** $y = (x + 4)^2$

   d $y = x^4 - 2x^2 + 5x^{-3}$ **e** $y = 2x^2(x^3 - 3x^{-1})$ **f** $y = x(x - 2)(x - 3)$

   g $y = (x^2 - 3)(x - 2)$ **h** $y = 3 + 4\sqrt{x}$ **i** $y = \frac{3x^4 - x}{x^2}$

   j $y = \frac{3}{x^2} - \frac{1}{2\sqrt{x}}$ **k** $y = \frac{2x^2 - 6x}{2\sqrt{x}}$ **l** $y = \frac{9x^3 - 2x^2 + 6}{3x}$

6   Find $\frac{d^2y}{dx^2}$ in each case

   a $y = x^4$ **b** $y = x^3 - 7x^2 + 2$ **c** $4x - x^{-1} + 3x^{-2}$

   d $y = (x^2 - 3)^2$ **e** $y = 4x^{\frac{3}{2}} + 2x^{-\frac{1}{2}}$ **f** $y = \frac{4x^2 - 5x + \sqrt{x}}{2x}$

7   Find the gradient of each curve at the point where $x = 2$.

    a $y = 3x^2$ **b** $y = x^3 - 9x$ **c** $y = x^2 + 6x^{-1}$

8   Find the gradient of each curve at the point where $x = {}^-1$.

    a $y = 2x^3$ **b** $y = x^2 + x^{-2}$ **c** $y = (x + 3)(x + 4)$

9   Find an equation of the tangent to each curve at the point with the given x-coordinate.

    a $y = x^2;$ $x = 1$ **b** $y = x^3 - 5x;$ $x = 2$

    c $y = x^2 + 6x + 3;$ $x = {}^-3$ **d** $y = 4 - x^2;$ $x = 5$

    e $y = 2\sqrt{x};$ $x = 16$ **f** $y = x - \frac{2}{x};$ $x = 2$

10 Find an equation of the normal to each curve at the point with the given x-coordinate.

    a $y = x^2;$ $x = 2$ **b** $y = 3 - 5x - x^2;$ $x = {}^-3$

    c $y = (x - 2)^2;$ $x = 3$ **d** $y = 5x^2 - x^3;$ $x = 4$

    e $y = 3x - \frac{1}{2}x^3;$ $x = {}^-1$ **f** $y = 6x^{\frac{1}{2}} - 18x^{-\frac{1}{2}};$ $x = 9$

11 Find in each case any values of x for which $\dfrac{dy}{dx} = 0$.

    a $y = x^2 + 3x$ **b** $y = x^3 - 27x$ **c** $y = 2x^3 + 3x^2 - 12x$

    d $y = x + 4x^{-1}$ **e** $y = x^3 - 2x^2 + 5$ **f** $y = 7 + 4x + 2x^2 - x^3$

12 Find the set of values for which f(x) is increasing.

    a $f(x) \equiv x^2 - 3x - 7$ **b** $f(x) \equiv x^3 - 3x^2$ **c** $f(x) \equiv x^3 + 9x^2 + 15x$

13 Find the set of values for which f(t) is decreasing.

    a $f(t) \equiv 3t^3 - t + 4$ **b** $f(t) \equiv t(t^2 - 9t - 21)$ **c** $f(x) \equiv 5 + t^2 - t^3$

14 Find the coordinates of the stationary point on the curve $y = x^2 + 4x - 1$

    a by completing the square,   **b** by using differentiation.

15 Find the coordinates of any stationary points on each curve. Find whether each stationary point is a maximum, minimum or point of inflexion.

    a $y = 4x^2 + 8x - 5$ **b** $y = x^2 - 5x + 7$ **c** $y = x^3 - 12x$

    d $y = 6 + 3x^2 - x^3$ **e** $y = 4 - x^3$ **f** $y = x^4 - 4x^3 + 4x^2$

    g $y = 4x + \dfrac{1}{x}$ **h** $y = 6x^{\frac{1}{2}} - x$ **i** $y = 16x - \dfrac{1}{x^2}$

16 Sketch each curve labelling the coordinates of any stationary points.

    a $y = 3x^3 - 9x - 2$ **b** $y = x^3 + 7x^2 - 5x$ **c** $y = 1 + 24x + 3x^2 - x^3$

17 $$f(x) \equiv x^2 - 6x - 1.$$

   a Find $f'(x)$.

   b Find the equation of the normal to the curve $y = f(x)$ at the point $(2, {}^-9)$

18 The height above ground, h metres, of a ball t seconds after being thrown upwards
     is given by $h = 8t - 5t^2$.

   a Find the rate at which the ball is gaining height when $t = 0.5$

   b Find the maximum height reached by the ball.

19 $$f(x) \equiv x^3 - 2x^2 + 3x + 5.$$

   a Find $f'(x)$.

   b Find the exact coordinates of the points on the curve $y = f(x)$ at which the
       gradient is 2.

20

x cm

y cm

   The diagram shows a thin rectangular picture frame measuring x cm by y cm.

   Given that the perimeter of the frame is to be 72 cm,

   a show that $y = 36 - x$,

   b find an expression in terms of x for the area, A cm^2, enclosed by the frame,

   c show that the largest value of A occurs when the frame is a square.

21 **a** Find the coordinates of the points where the curve $y = 4x - x^2$ crosses
       the x-axis.

   b Find the equation of the tangent to the curve $y = 4x - x^2$ at each of the points
       found in part **a**.

22 $$y = x + \frac{9}{x}$$

   a State any values of x for which y is undefined.

   b Find the coordinates of any stationary points on the curve $y = x + \frac{9}{x}$ and
       determine their nature.

   c Sketch the curve $y = x + \frac{9}{x}$.

23 The size of a spinning cube on a computer screen saver varies so that the length of
     one side, l cm, t seconds after the start, is given by $l = \frac{1}{3}t^2 - 3t + 10$ for $0 \le t < 9$.

   a Find the rate at which l is changing when $t = 2$.

   b Find the smallest value of l.

Exercise 16E   Exam Practice

1   **a**   Find an equation of the tangent to the curve $y = 2 + 3x - 2x^2$ at
   the point A (2, 0).   **(4 marks)**

b   Find an equation of the tangent to the curve $y = 2 + 3x - 2x^2$ at
   the point B, where it meets the y-axis.   **(3 marks)**

c   Find the coordinates of the point C, where the tangents you have
   found in parts **a** and **b** intersect.   **(3 marks)**

2

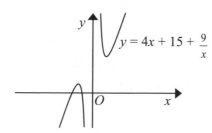

The diagram shows part of the curve $y = 4x + 15 + \dfrac{9}{x}$

a   Find the coordinates of the points where the curve intersects
   the x-axis.   **(4 marks)**

b   Find the coordinates of the turning points of the curve.   **(5 marks)**

3

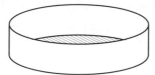

The diagram shows an open-topped cylindrical cake tin.

Given that the volume of the tin is to be 1000π cm^3,

a   find an expression for the height, h cm, of the tin in terms of
   the radius of the base of the tin, r cm.   **(2 marks)**

b   show that the area of metal, A cm^2, used in making the tin is
   given by $A = \pi r^2 + \dfrac{2000\pi}{r}$.   **(3 marks)**

Given that r can vary,

c   find the minimum value of A in terms of π,   **(6 marks)**

d   justify that your value is a minimum.   **(3 marks)**

4 $f(x) \equiv x^3 - x^2 + kx + 2.$

Given that $(x - 2)$ is a factor of $f(x)$,

a   find the value of the constant k,   **(2 marks)**

b   find exactly the set of values of x for which $f(x)$ is decreasing.   **(6 marks)**

5

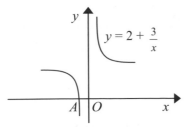

The diagram shows part of the curve $y = 2 + \frac{3}{x}$.

The curve intersects the x-axis at the point A.

a   Find the coordinates of the point A.   **(2 marks)**

b   Find an equation of the normal to the curve at the point A.   **(6 marks)**

c   Show that the normal intersects the curve again at the point
    with coordinates $(\frac{8}{3}, \frac{25}{8})$.   **(5 marks)**

6   The number of people in thousands, P, at an outdoor festival h hours
        after the gates open is modelled with the formula

$$P = 15h + 6h^2 - h^3, \text{ for } h \geq 0.$$

Using this model,

a   find an expression in terms of h for the rate at which P increases,   **(2 marks)**

b   show that the population is increasing most rapidly when $h = 2$,   **(3 marks)**

c   find the number of people entering the festival per minute when
    $h = 2$, assuming that no one is leaving.   **(3 marks)**

7

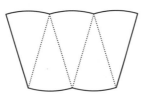

The diagram shows the shape of a new biscuit, consisting of five
circular sectors, each of radius r cm and angle θ radians.

a   Find expressions in terms of r and θ for the perimeter and
    area of the shape.   **(4 marks)**

Given that the area of the shape is to be 40 cm^2,

b   show that the perimeter of the shape, P cm, can be expressed as

$$P = 20\theta^{\frac{1}{2}} + 80^{-\frac{1}{2}}.$$ **(4 marks)**

Given that θ can vary,

c   find the value of θ for which P is a minimum and find the
    corresponding value of P in the form $k\sqrt{10}$.   **(7 marks)**

Integration

Exercise 17S	Skills Practice

1   Integrate with respect to x.

a x^2	**b** x^8	**c** x^5	**d** x^{-2}	**e** x	**f** 4
g x^{-5}	**h** $3x^2$	**i** $8x^{-3}$	**j** $2x^4$	**k** $3x^{-2}$	**l** $7x^3$
m $x^{\frac{1}{2}}$	**n** $x^{\frac{1}{3}}$	**o** $x^{-\frac{3}{4}}$	**p** $5x^{\frac{2}{3}}$	**q** $3x^{-\frac{3}{5}}$	**r** $\frac{1}{3}x^{-\frac{5}{6}}$

2   Integrate with respect to r.

a r^3	**b** $4r$	**c** $2r^{-6}$	**d** 19	**e** $r^{\frac{8}{3}}$	**f** $2r^{-\frac{1}{5}}$
g $\sqrt{r}$	**h** $\frac{1}{r^2}$	**i** $\frac{3}{r^4}$	**j** $\frac{1}{2\sqrt{r}}$	**k** $\sqrt[3]{r^2}$	**l** $\frac{5}{\sqrt[4]{r}}$

3   Find $\int f(x)\ dx$

a $f(x) \equiv 3x^2 - 10x$ **b** $f(x) \equiv 8x^3 + 2$ **c** $f(x) \equiv 15x^4 + 6x^2 - 4$

d $f(x) \equiv 7 - x^2$ **e** $f(x) \equiv 4x^3 + 2x^2 - 1$ **f** $f(x) \equiv 6x^2 + 5x + 3$

g $f(x) \equiv 6x + x^{-2}$ **h** $f(x) \equiv x^5 - x^3 + 9x^{-4}$ **i** $f(x) \equiv x(x + 3)$

j $f(x) \equiv (x - 4)(x - 1)$ **k** $f(x) \equiv x(3x^4 - 2x^{-4})$ **l** $f(x) \equiv (x - 2)^3$

4   Find

a $\int (8x^2 + x - 1)\ dx$ **b** $\int (2t^3 + t^2 + t)\ dt$ **c** $\int (x + 2)^2\ dx$

d $\int (x^{\frac{3}{2}} + x^{\frac{1}{2}})\ dx$ **e** $\int (\frac{1}{2}x^3 - x^4)\ dx$ **f** $\int (r + 3)(r^2 - 1)\ dr$

g $\int (2x^{\frac{4}{3}} - 5x^{\frac{1}{3}})\ dx$ **h** $\int (x^{-\frac{1}{2}} + 6x^{-3})\ dx$ **i** $\int (4 - \sqrt{x})\ dx$

j $\int 3y^{\frac{1}{2}}(7y^2 - y^{\frac{1}{2}})\ dy$ **k** $\int \frac{x^3 + 4x}{2x}\ dx$ **l** $\int \frac{2x^6 + x^3 - 6}{3x^2}\ dx$

5   Given $\frac{dy}{dx}$ and that $y = 3$ when $x = 2$, find y in terms of x in each case.

a $\frac{dy}{dx} = 2x + 3$ **b** $\frac{dy}{dx} = 3x^2 - 4x + 3$ **c** $\frac{dy}{dx} = x^3 + 12x^{-3}$

6   Find $f(x)$ in each case given $f'(x)$ and the coordinates of a point on $y = f(x)$.

a $f'(x) \equiv 8x - 7;$ $(1, 2)$ **b** $f'(x) \equiv 3x^2 - 2;$ $(2, {}^-3)$

c $f'(x) \equiv 1 - 8x - 3x^2;$ $({}^-3, 0)$ **d** $f'(x) \equiv 2x^3 - 9x + 6;$ $(2, {}^-4)$

e $f'(x) \equiv 3x^{\frac{1}{2}} - 2x^{-\frac{1}{2}};$ $(4, 13)$ **f** $f'(x) \equiv (x - 3)(3x + 1);$ $(5, 8)$

7   Evaluate

a $\int_5^8 (2x+3)\ dx$ b $\int_2^6 (y-5)\ dy$ c $\int_0^3 (3x^2-6)\ dx$

d $\int_{-1}^2 (4t^3-t^2+2)\ dt$ e $\int_4^9 (3x^{\frac{1}{2}}+5x^{-\frac{1}{2}})\ dx$ f $\int_{-4}^{-2} (6-3y-y^2)\ dy$

g $\int_1^2 (5r^{-2}-4r^{-3})\ dr$ h $\int_1^8 2x^{-\frac{1}{3}}(5x-1)\ dx$ i $\int_0^1 (x+2)(x^{\frac{1}{2}}-1)\ dx$

8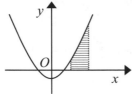

The shaded region on the diagram is enclosed by the curve $y = 3x^2 - 1$, the
ordinates $x = 1$ and $x = 2$, and the x-axis.

Find the area of the shaded region.

9   a Evaluate $\int_1^3 (3x^2-12x)\ dx$.

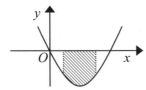

The shaded region on the diagram is enclosed by the curve $y = 3x^2 - 12x$, the
ordinates $x = 1$ and $x = 3$, and the x-axis.

b Use your answer to part **a** to write down the area of the shaded region.

10   a Find the coordinates of the points where the curve $y = 4x - x^2$
intersects the x-axis and sketch the curve.

b Find the area enclosed by the curve and the x-axis.

11   Find the area enclosed by the given curve and the x-axis.

a $y = 18x - 3x^2$ b $y = x^2 - 4x + 3$ c $y = x^3 + 3x^2$

12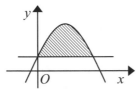

The diagram shows the line $y = 1$ and the curve $y = 1 + 6x - 3x^2$.

a Find the coordinates of the points where the line and curve intersect.

b Find the area of the shaded region enclosed by the line and curve.

13

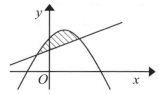

The diagram shows the line $y = x + 7$ and the curve $y = 10 + 3x - x^2$.

a Find the coordinates of the points where the line and curve intersect.

b Find the area of the shaded region enclosed by the line and curve.

14 On the same set of coordinate axes sketch the given line and curve.

Hence find the area of the region enclosed by the line and curve.

a $y = x$	**b** $y = 6x - 15$	**c** $y = 2x - 1$
$y = 3x - x^2$	$y = 3x^2 - 15$	$y = 2x^2 - 16x + 35$

15

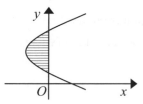

The diagram shows the curve $x = y^2 - 5y + 4$.

a Find the coordinates of the points where the curve intersects the y-axis

b Find the area of the shaded region enclosed by the curve and the y-axis

16 Find the area enclosed by the given curve and the y-axis.

a $x = 1 - y^2$ **b** $x = 3y^2 - 15y$ **c** $x = 2y^2 - 3y - 2$

17 Find the area of the shaded region in each case.

a

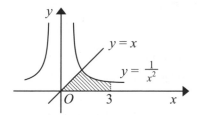

b

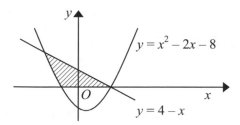

Exercise 17E   Exam Practice

1 $f(x) \equiv x(x^2 + 2)(2x - 3x^{-1}).$

   a Express $f(x)$ in the form $ax^4 + bx^2 + c$.   **(3 marks)**

   b Evaluate $\int_0^2 f(x)\ dx$, giving your answer as an exact fraction.   **(5 marks)**

2

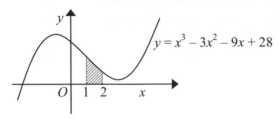

The diagram shows part of the curve $y = x^3 - 3x^2 - 9x + 28$.

   a Find the coordinates of the stationary points on the curve.   **(5 marks)**

   b Find the area of the shaded region enclosed by the curve, the
ordinates $x = 1$ and $x = 2$, and the x-axis.   **(5 marks)**

3 $f(x) \equiv 6x^{\frac{1}{2}} - x^{-\frac{1}{2}}.$

   a Find $\int f(x)\ dx$.   **(3 marks)**

   b Evaluate $\int_1^3 f(x)\ dx$, giving your answer in the form $a + b\sqrt{3}$.   **(4 marks)**

4

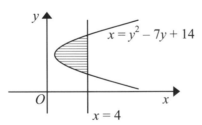

The diagram shows the line $x = 4$ and the curve $x = y^2 - 7y + 14$.

   a Find the coordinates of the points where the line and
curve intersect.   **(4 marks)**

   b Find the area of the shaded region enclosed by the line and
the curve.   **(6 marks)**

5 The curve $y = f(x)$ passes through the point $(2, 9)$.

   Given also that $f'(x) \equiv 1 + \dfrac{2}{x^2}$,

   a find $f(x)$,   **(4 marks)**

   b solve the equation $f(x) - 0$, giving your answers in surd form.   **(5 marks)**

6

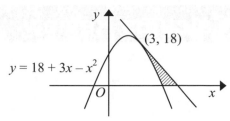

The diagram shows part of the curve $y = 18 + 3x - x^2$.

a Find an equation of the tangent to the curve at the point (3, 18). **(5 marks)**

b Find the area of the shaded region enclosed by the curve, the tangent and the positive x-axis. **(7 marks)**

7 **a** By letting $u = x^{\frac{1}{2}}$, or otherwise, find the values of x for which

$$x - 3x^{\frac{1}{2}} + 2 = 0 \qquad \textbf{(4 marks)}$$

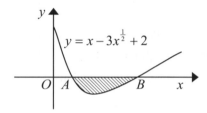

The diagram shows the curve $y = x - 3x^{\frac{1}{2}} + 2$ which intersects the x-axis at the points A and B.

b State the coordinates of the points A and B. **(1 mark)**

c Find the area of the shaded region enclosed by the curve and the x-axis. **(5 marks)**

8

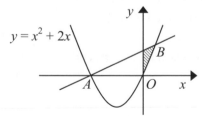

The diagram shows the curve $y = x^2 + 2x$ which intersects the x-axis at the origin, O, and the point A, with coordinates ($^-2$, 0).

a Find an equation of the normal to the curve at A. **(5 marks)**

b Find the coordinates of the point B, where the normal again intersects the curve. **(4 marks)**

c Show that the area of the shaded region enclosed by the section of the curve OB, the normal and the y-axis is $\frac{13}{48}$. **(7 marks)**

Geometry and Calculus Review

Exercise 18E   Exam Practice

1 $$f(x) \equiv 6 + 48x - 9x^2 - x^3.$$

Find the set of values of x for which $f(x)$ is increasing. **(6 marks)**

2 **a** Find $\int 16x + \dfrac{2}{x^3} \, dx$. **(3 marks)**

Given that $\dfrac{dy}{dx} = 16x + \dfrac{2}{x^3}$ and that when $x = \frac{1}{2}$, $y = 5$

b find an expression for y in terms of x. **(3 marks)**

3 The line l passes through the points A (6, 0) and B (10, 8).

a Find an equation of the line l. **(3 marks)**

The line m has the equation $x + 3y - 20 = 0$.

Given that the lines l and m intersect at the point C,

b find in the form $k\sqrt{5}$ the length OC, where O is the origin. **(6 marks)**

4

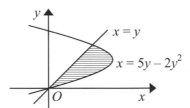

The diagram shows the line $x = y$ and the curve $x = 5y - 2y^2$.

a Find the coordinates of the points where the line and curve intersect. **(3 marks)**

b Find the area of the shaded region enclosed by the line and the curve. **(6 marks)**

5 $$f(x) \equiv 3x^3 - k^2x + k^3.$$

a Find in terms of k the values of x for which $f'(x) = 0$. **(4 marks)**

b Find in terms of k the coordinates of the stationary points on the curve $y = f(x)$. **(3 marks)**

c Show that the gradient of the line joining the stationary points you found in part **b** is $-\dfrac{2k^2}{3}$. **(3 marks)**

6
$$y = x^{\frac{3}{2}} - 5.$$

a Express y^2 in descending powers of x.   **(3 marks)**

b Evaluate $\displaystyle\int_{1}^{4} y^2 \, dx$.   **(5 marks)**

7
$$f(x) \equiv x + x^2 - 2x^3.$$

a Find an equation of the tangent to the curve $y = f(x)$ at the point $P\,(1, 0)$.   **(4 marks)**

b Find an equation of the tangent to the curve $y = f(x)$ at the origin O.   **(2 marks)**

The tangents to the curve $y = f(x)$ at O and P meet at the point Q.

c Find the coordinates of Q.   **(3 marks)**

d Show that $\angle OQP = 63.4°$ correct to 1 decimal place.   **(4 marks)**

8 The line l has a gradient of $\sqrt{3}$ and passes through the points $A\,(2\sqrt{3}, 4)$ and $B\,(4, k)$.

a Show that $k = 4\sqrt{3} - 2$.   **(3 marks)**

b Find the coordinates of the mid-point of AB.   **(2 marks)**

c Find in the form $a + b\sqrt{3}$, the area of a square, one side of which is AB.   **(4 marks)**

9

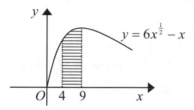

The diagram shows part of the curve $y = 6x^{\frac{1}{2}} - x$.

a Find the coordinates of the maximum point on the curve.   **(5 marks)**

b Find the area of the shaded region enclosed by the curve, the ordinates $x = 4$ and $x = 9$, and the x-axis.   **(5 marks)**

10 P is the point with coordinates $(^-1, 5)$. The x-coordinate of the point Q is k and it lies on the line l which has equation $y = 12 - 3x$.

a Show that $PQ^2 = 10k^2 - 40k + 50$.   **(4 marks)**

b Find the minimum value of PQ.   **(4 marks)**

c State the size of the angle in degrees between the line PQ and the line l corresponding to this minimum value of PQ.   **(1 mark)**

11

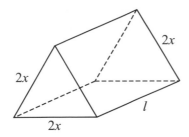

The diagram shows a solid prism of length l cm. The cross-section of the prism is an equilateral triangle of side $2x$ cm.

Given that the surface area of the prism is $150\sqrt{3}$ cm^2,

   a find an expression for l in terms of x,   **(6 marks)**

   b show that the volume of the prism, V cm^3, is given by

$$V = 75x - x^3.$$ **(3 marks)**

Given that x can vary,

   c find the maximum value of V,   **(4 marks)**

   d justify that the value you have found is a maximum.   **(2 marks)**

12 A and B are the points with coordinates $(18, 1)$ and $(10, {}^-3)$ respectively.

   a Find the coordinates of the mid-point of AB.   **(2 marks)**

   b Find an equation of the perpendicular bisector of AB.   **(4 marks)**

   C is the point with coordinates $(0, 7)$.

   c Find an equation of the perpendicular bisector of BC.   **(4 marks)**

   Given that A, B and C are points on the circumference of a circle,

   d find the coordinates of the centre of the circle.   **(4 marks)**

13

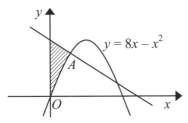

The diagram shows part of the curve $y = 8x - x^2$ and the normal to the curve at the point A with coordinates $(3, 15)$.

   a Find the equation of the normal in the form $ax + by + c = 0$.   **(6 marks)**

   b Show that the area of the shaded region enclosed by the curve, the normal and the y-axis is $\frac{81}{4}$.   **(7 marks)**

Proof

Exercise 19S   Skills Practice

1   Prove that for all real values of x

    a $x^2 + 2x + 1 \geq 0$ **b** $x^2 + 4 \geq 4x$ **c** $x(2 - x) \leq 1$

    d $9x^2 + 1 \geq 6x$ **e** $(x + 1)^2 \geq 4x$ **f** $12x \leq 36 + x^2$

    g $(x + 1)^2 + (x - 1)^2 \geq 2$ **h** $2x + 9 \leq (x + 5)^2$ **i** $(x - 2)^2 \geq 1 - \frac{1}{3}x^2$

2   Prove that for all real values of a and b

    a $a^2 + 2ab + b^2 \geq 0$ **b** $a^2 + b^2 \geq 2ab$ **c** $a^2 + 4b^2 \geq 4ab$

    d $24ab - 16a^2 \leq 9b^2$ **e** $(a + b)^2 \geq 3a(2b - a)$ **f** $a^4 \geq 4b(a^2 - b)$

3   Prove that the equation

    a $x^2 + 2x + k = 0$ only has real roots if $k \leq 1$

    b $x^2 - 6x + k = 0$ only has repeated roots if $k = 9$

    c $2x^2 + x + k = 0$ has no real roots only if $k > \frac{1}{8}$

    d $x^2 + 4x + k^2 = 0$ only has real and distinct roots if $^-2 < k < 2$

    e $x^2 - 2x + k + 1 = 0$ only has real roots if $k \leq 0$

    f $kx^2 + 8x + 2k = 0$ only has repeated roots if $k = \pm 2\sqrt{2}$

    g $x^2 + 2px + q = 0$ has no real roots only if $q > p^2$

    h $px^2 + 6x + 3q = 0$ only has real and distinct roots if $pq < 3$

4   Prove from first principles that

    a $1 + 2 + 3 + 4 + \ldots + (n - 1) + n = \frac{1}{2}n(n + 1)$

    b $1 + 3 + 5 + 7 + \ldots + (2n - 3) + (2n - 1) = n^2$

    c $n + (n + 1) + (n + 2) + (n + 3) + \ldots + (3n - 1) + 3n = 2n(2n + 1)$

    d $2 + 4 + 8 + 16 + \ldots + 2^{n-1} + 2^n = 2^{n+1} - 2$

    e $\frac{1}{9} + \frac{1}{3} + 1 + 3 + \ldots + 3^{n-1} + 3^n = \frac{1}{2}(3^{n+1} - \frac{1}{9})$

    f $1 + \frac{1}{2} + \frac{1}{4} + \frac{1}{8} + \ldots + \frac{1}{2^{n-1}} + \frac{1}{2^n} = 2 - \frac{1}{2^n}$

5   Prove that

    a $2 + 2\sin x - \cos^2 x \equiv (\sin x + 1)^2$ **b** $\sin^2 x - (\sin x \cos x)^2 \equiv \sin^4 x$

    c $\sin x \tan x \equiv \frac{1}{\cos x} - \cos x$ **d** $\frac{\sin x \cos x}{\tan x} \equiv 1 - \sin^2 x$

    e $1 - \tan^2 x \equiv 2 - \frac{1}{\cos^2 x}$ **f** $(2\sin x - 1)^2 + 4\sin x \equiv 5 - 4\cos^2 x$

Exercise 19E	Exam Practice

1 Prove that for all real values of x and y

  a $(3x + 2)^2 + (x - 6)^2 \geq 40$ **(3 marks)**

  b $x^2 + 25y^2 \geq 10xy$ **(3 marks)**

2 **a** Prove that the equation

$$p^2x^2 + (2p - 1)x + 1 = 0$$

  only has real solutions if $p \leq \frac{1}{4}$. **(3 marks)**

  b Prove that the equation

$$x^2 + kx + k - 1 = 0$$

  has real solutions for all values of k. **(3 marks)**

3 **a** Prove that the sum, S_n, of the first n terms of an arithmetic series with first term a and common difference d is given by

$$S_n = \tfrac{1}{2} n[2a + (n - 1)d].$$ **(4 marks)**

  b Given that

$$\sum_{r=1}^{20} (kr + 2) = 670,$$

  find the value of the constant k. **(5 marks)**

4 The line l passes through the points $A\,(^-6, 4)$ and $B\,(2, 3)$.

  a Find the equation of the line l in the form $ax + by + c = 0$. **(3 marks)**

  b Prove that $\angle AOB = 90°$, where O is the origin. **(4 marks)**

5 Given that the equation $2px^2 - 4x + q = 0$ has real and distinct roots,

  a show that $pq < 2$. **(3 marks)**

  Given also that p and q are positive integers,

  b find the values of p and q, **(2 marks)**

  c solve the equation, giving your answers in exact form. **(4 marks)**

6 **a** Prove that

$$(2\sin x + \cos x)^2 - (\sin x + 2\cos x)^2 \equiv 3(\sin^2 x - \cos^2 x).$$ **(3 marks)**

  b Hence find the values of x in the interval $0 \leq x \leq 2\pi$ for which

$$(2\sin x + \cos x)^2 - (\sin x + 2\cos x)^2 = 0$$

  giving your answers in terms of π. **(5 marks)**

7   a   By completing the square, derive the formula for the solutions
         to the equation
$$ax^2 + bx + c = 0.$$
                                                          (6 marks)

     b   Find in the form $a + b\sqrt{5}$ the solutions to the equation
$$x^2 - 12x - 9 = 0.$$
                                                          (4 marks)

8    $$f(x) \equiv x^2 + 2ax + b^2.$$

     Given that the equation $f(x) = 0$ has repeated real roots,

     a   prove that $a = \pm b$,   **(3 marks)**

     b   find in terms of a the coordinates of the minimum point on the
         curve $y = f(x)$.   **(3 marks)**

9   a   Prove that the sum, S_n, of the first n terms of a geometric series
         with first term a and common ratio r is given by
$$S_n = \frac{a(r^n - 1)}{r - 1}.$$
                                                          (4 marks)

     b   The first two terms of a geometric series are 4 and 5 respectively.

         Find the sum of the first 12 terms of the series correct to
         1 decimal place.   **(3 marks)**

10   a   State the condition for which the equation
$$ax^2 + bx + c = 0$$
         will have real roots.   **(1 mark)**

     b   Prove that the equation
$$x^2 + kx - 2x + k + 6 = 0$$
         only has real roots if $k \leq {}^-2$ or $k \geq 10$.   **(6 marks)**

11   $$f(x) \equiv x^2 - 6x + 11.$$

     a   Prove that the line $3x - 4y - 6 = 0$ does not intersect the
         curve $y = f(x)$.   **(4 marks)**

     b   Prove that the line $2x + y - 7 = 0$ is a tangent to the curve $y = f(x)$.   **(4 marks)**

12   a   Find an expression in terms of a, b and n for
$$\sum_{r=1}^{n} (ar + b).$$
                                                          (4 marks)

     b   Hence, prove that for all values of a, b and n,
$$\sum_{r=1}^{n} (ar + b) \equiv a\sum_{r=1}^{n} r + nb.$$
                                                          (4 marks)

Course Review

Exercise 20E   Exam Practice

1   Find the set of values of y for which

$$y(4y - 15) < (y - 2)^2.$$ **(5 marks)**

2 $$f(x) \equiv 3x^3 - 11x^2 + 8x + 4.$$

   a   Show that $(x - 2)$ is a factor of f(x).   **(2 marks)**

   b   Hence, express f(x) as the product of linear factors.   **(5 marks)**

   c   Find f$'(x)$.   **(2 marks)**

   d   Find the x-coordinates of the turning points of the curve $y = f(x)$.   **(3 marks)**

   e   Sketch the graph of $y = f(x)$.   **(3 marks)**

3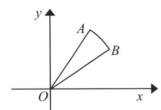

The diagram shows part of a circle, centre O, of radius r.
The points A (3, 4) and B (4, 3) lie on the circumference of the
circle such that $\angle AOB = \theta$ radians.

   a   Calculate r.   **(2 marks)**

   b   Find θ correct to 2 decimal places.   **(4 marks)**

   c   Find an equation of the line AB.   **(3 marks)**

   d   Show that the perpendicular bisector of AB passes through O.   **(4 marks)**

4   Given that $y = Ax^2 + \dfrac{B}{x}$,

   show that $\dfrac{d^2 y}{dx^2} = \dfrac{2y}{x^2}$.   **(6 marks)**

5   The curve $y = k\sin\left(x - \frac{\pi}{2}\right)$, where x is measured in radians, passes
through the point with coordinates $\left(\frac{2\pi}{3}, \frac{3}{2}\right)$.

   a   Find the value of k.   **(3 marks)**

   b   Write down the maximum value of y.   **(1 mark)**

   c   Find the smallest positive value of x for which y is a maximum.   **(4 marks)**

6   **a**   Prove that for all real values of x,

       i $x^2 + 1 \geq 2x$

       ii $4x^2 \geq 3(4x - 3)$ **(6 marks)**

    b   Prove that for all real values of p and q,

$$(p - 2q)^2 \geq q(2p - 5q).$$ **(3 marks)**

7   A car hire company opened on 1st January 1995 with one new car valued at £12 000. During each year, the car loses 25% of its value at the start of that year.

    a   Show that the car was worth £6750 on 1st January 1997.   **(2 marks)**

On the 1st January each year, the company adds a new £12 000 car to its fleet. All the cars depreciate in the same manner as the first one.

    b   Find the value of the whole fleet, correct to the nearest pound, on 1st January 2001.   **(5 marks)**

The value of the whole fleet first exceeds £45 000 on 1st January in the company's nth year of trading.

    c   Show that n is given by the solution to the inequality

$$\left(\tfrac{3}{4}\right)^n < \tfrac{1}{16}.$$ **(4 marks)**

8   **a**   Find the values of x in the interval $0 \leq x < 360°$ for which

$$5 \sin x - 2 = 0$$

       giving your answers correct to an appropriate level of accuracy.   **(4 marks)**

    b   Sketch the curve $y = 5 \sin x - 2$ for x in the interval $0 \leq x < 360°$.   **(4 marks)**

    c   State the set of values of x in the interval $0 \leq x < 360°$ for which

$$5 \sin x - 2 > 0.$$ **(2 marks)**

9

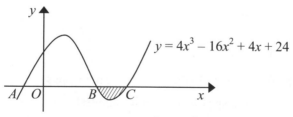

The diagram shows the curve $y = 4x^3 - 16x^2 + 4x + 24$ which intersects the x-axis at the points A, B and C.

Given that B and C have coordinates $(2, 0)$ and $(3, 0)$ respectively,

    a   find the coordinates of the point A,   **(5 marks)**

    b   show that the area of the shaded region enclosed by the curve and the x-axis between the points B and C is $\tfrac{7}{3}$.   **(6 marks)**

10   **a**   Factorise the expression

$$2ab - b + 2a - 1.$$ **(2 marks)**

b   Hence, find the values of x in the interval $0 \le x \le 2\pi$ for which

$$2\cos x \sin x - \sin x + 2\cos x - 1 = 0,$$

giving your answers in terms of π.   **(5 marks)**

11   The points A (3, 0) and C (4, 3) are the opposite vertices of a square $ABCD$.

a   Find the exact distance AC.   **(2 marks)**

b   Find the area of the square $ABCD$.   **(4 marks)**

c   Find an equation of the line AC.   **(3 marks)**

d   Find the equation of the line BD in the form $ax + by + c = 0$.   **(4 marks)**

12

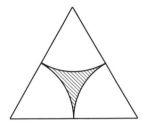

Three identical circular sectors of radius r and angle $60°$ are arranged as shown in the diagram. The straight edges of the sectors together form an equilateral triangle of side $2r$.

a   Find, in terms of r, the exact perimeter of the shaded region enclosed by the three sectors.   **(3 marks)**

b   Show that the area of the shaded region enclosed by the three sectors is $r^2(\sqrt{3} - \frac{\pi}{2})$.   **(5 marks)**

13 $$f(x) \equiv 3\sqrt{3}\, x^{\frac{1}{2}} + 6x^{-\frac{1}{2}}.$$

a   Find f(3) in the form $m + n\sqrt{3}$ where m and n are integers.   **(3 marks)**

b   Evaluate, giving your answer exactly in its simplest form,

$$\int_{1}^{3} f(x)\ dx.$$ **(5 marks)**

14   Given that

$$(a + b\sqrt{2})^2 = 17 - 12\sqrt{2},$$

find the two possible integer values of a, and the corresponding values of b.   **(7 marks)**

15 Given that $x = 2p + p^{-1}$ and $y = p - 3p^{-1}$, find and simplify expressions in terms of p for

    a $x^2 - 4$,   **(2 marks)**

    b $x^2 y^2$.   **(5 marks)**

16 The first three terms of an arithmetic series are $(p - 5)$, $(p^2 + 1)$ and $(5p + 3)$ respectively.

    a Find the two possible values of p.   **(5 marks)**

    b Show that the ratio of the sum of the first three terms of the series for the smaller value of p to the sum of the first three terms of the series for the larger value of p is $2 : 5$.   **(4 marks)**

17 $$y = 3x^{\frac{5}{2}} - 5x^{\frac{3}{2}}, \; x > 0.$$

    a Show that $\dfrac{dy}{dx}$ can be written in the form $Ax^{\frac{1}{2}}(x-1)$ where A is an exact fraction to be found.   **(3 marks)**

    b Hence, or otherwise, find the coordinates of the turning point of the curve $y = 3x^{\frac{5}{2}} - 5x^{\frac{3}{2}}$ and determine the nature of this point.   **(3 marks)**

    c Show that $\displaystyle\int_{1}^{4} y \; dx = 46\frac{6}{7}$.   **(5 marks)**

18   **a** Sketch on the same diagram the curves $y = \sin 2x$ and $y = \cos 2x$, for x in the interval $0 \leq x \leq 2\pi$.   **(4 marks)**

    b Find, for x in the interval $0 \leq x \leq 2\pi$, the exact coordinates of the points where the two curves intersect.   **(8 marks)**

19   **a** Prove that the equation
$$x^2 + kx + 3x + k^2 = 0$$
    only has real roots if
$$k^2 - 2k - 3 \leq 0$$
                                                      (3 marks)

    b Hence find the set of values of k for which the equation
$$x^2 + kx + 3x + k^2 = 0$$
    has real roots.   **(3 marks)**

20 $$f(x) \equiv 2x^3 + 5x^2 - x - 6.$$

    a Show that $f(x)$ can be expressed in the form $(x - 1)(x + a)(bx + c)$ where a, b and c are integers to be found.   **(5 marks)**

    b Find the x-coordinates of the turning points of the curve $y = f(x)$, giving your answers correct to 3 significant figures.   **(4 marks)**

    c Sketch the curve $y = f(x)$.   **(3 marks)**

21   Find the pairs of values (x, y) which satisfy the simultaneous equations

$$2x^2 + 3xy - 4y + 2 = 0$$
$$x - y + 3 = 0$$

(6 marks)

22   **a**   Sketch the curve $y = \tan 4\theta$ for θ in the interval $0 \le \theta < 180°$.   **(3 marks)**

b   Hence, determine the number of solutions to the equation
$\tan 4\theta = k$, in the interval $0 \le \theta < 180°$ for any value of k.   **(1 mark)**

c   Find the values of θ in the interval $0 \le \theta < 180°$ for which

$$\sin 4\theta = \sqrt{3}\cos 4\theta.$$

(5 marks)

23   By letting $x = t^{\frac{1}{4}}$, or otherwise, solve the equation

$$6t^{\frac{1}{2}} - 13t^{\frac{1}{4}} + 6 = 0.$$

(6 marks)

24 $$f(x) \equiv 4x^2 - 12x + 11.$$

a   Show that $f(x)$ can be written in the form $(Ax + B)^2 + C$ where
A, B and C are integers to be found and $A > 0$.   **(5 marks)**

b   Hence, or otherwise, find the coordinates of the vertex of $y = f(x)$.   **(2 marks)**

25

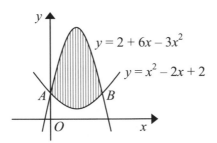

The diagram shows the curves $y = x^2 - 2x + 2$ and $y = 2 + 6x - 3x^2$
which intersect at the points A and B.

a   Find the coordinates of the points A and B.   **(4 marks)**

b   Find the area of the shaded region enclosed by the two curves.   **(7 marks)**

26 $$f(x) \equiv 2x - 3 + \frac{8}{x}.$$

Find the set of values of x for which $f(x)$ is increasing.   **(5 marks)**

27   The recurring decimal 0.212121... can be written as the series

$$\frac{21}{100} + \frac{21}{10000} + \frac{21}{1000000} + \dots$$

a   Name this type of series.   **(1 mark)**

b   State the condition for which this type of series converges.   **(2 marks)**

c   By finding the sum to infinity of the series, express 0.212121...
as an exact fraction in its lowest terms.   **(3 marks)**

28 Prove that the equation
$$2\cos^2 x + \sin x + 8 = 0$$
has no real solutions. **(6 marks)**

29

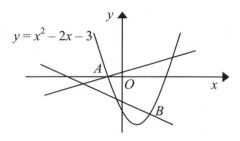

$y = x^2 - 2x - 3$

The diagram shows the curve $y = x^2 - 2x - 3$ and the normals to the curve at the points $A\ (^-1, 0)$ and $B\ (2, ^-3)$.

a Show that the normal to the curve at A has equation $y = \frac{1}{4}x + \frac{1}{4}$. **(5 marks)**

b Find the equation of the normal to the curve at B in the form $ax + by + c = 0$. **(4 marks)**

c Find the coordinates of the point where the two normals intersect. **(3 marks)**

30 $$f(x) \equiv x^2 - 5x + 7.$$

a Express $f(x)$ in the form $(x - a)^2 + b$ where a and b are positive constants to be found. **(3 marks)**

b Hence, find the maximum value of $\dfrac{1}{f(x)}$. **(3 marks)**

31 The sum of the first n terms of a geometric series, S_n, is given by
$$S_n = k^n - 1.$$

a Find an expression in terms of k for the second term of the series. **(4 marks)**

Given that the second term of the series is 6,

b show that one possible value of k is 3 and find the other possible value. **(4 marks)**

c Find the value of the fifth term of the series when $k = 3$. **(4 marks)**

32 a Find the values of $\sin x$ and $\cos y$ which satisfy the simultaneous equations
$$8\sin x + 6\cos y = 1$$
$$3\sin x - 5\cos y = 4$$ **(4 marks)**

b Hence, solve these simultaneous equations for x in the interval $0 \le x < 180°$ and y in the interval $0 \le y < 180°$. **(4 marks)**

33 $f(x) \equiv 2x^4 - 4x^3 + 3x^2 - 2x + 1.$

   a Show that $f(\sqrt{3}) = 14(2 - \sqrt{3})$.   **(3 marks)**

   b Find $f'(x)$ and show that $f'(1) = 0$.   **(4 marks)**

   c Prove that $x = 1$ is the only real solution of $f'(x) = 0$.   **(4 marks)**

   d Solve the equation $f''(x) = 0$ **(4 marks)**

34

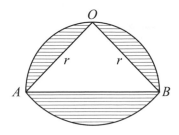

The diagram shows triangle OAB in which $OA = OB = r$, and three circular arcs OA, OB and AB. The arcs OA and OB together form a semicircle with AB as its diameter. The arc AB has centre O and radius r.

   a Find an expression for the length AB in terms of r.   **(2 marks)**

   b Show that the total area of the three shaded segments is $r^2(\frac{\pi}{2} - 1)$.   **(7 marks)**

35   Given that $a > 1$, find the value of a such that

$$\int_1^a (4x - 1) \; dx = 2.$$ **(6 marks)**

36   Given that the x-axis is a tangent to the curve with equation

$$y = 3p + 6x + qx^2,$$

   a Prove that $pq = 3$.   **(3 marks)**

   Given also that the curve passes through the point $(1, {}^-4)$,

   b find the two possible values of p and the corresponding values of q.   **(6 marks)**

37   **a** Show that

$$\sum_{r=1}^{n} (2r - 7) = n(n - 6).$$ **(4 marks)**

   b Hence, or otherwise, find the positive value of n for which

$$\sum_{r=1}^{n} (2r - 7) = \sum_{r=n}^{n+7} (2r - 7)$$ **(5 marks)**

THE LIBRARY
TOWER HAMLETS COLLEGE
POPLAR HIGH STREET
LONDON E14 0AF
Tel: 0207 510 7763

Answers

Exercise 1S   Skills Practice

1 **a** 1, 3, 9   **b** 1, 2, 7, 14
  c 1, 2, 3, 4, 6, 8, 12, 24   **d** 1, 41
  e 1, 2, 3, 4, 5, 6, 10, 12, 15, 20, 30, 60
  f 1, 2, 5, 10, 25, 50, 125, 250

2 **a** 4   **b** 7   **c** 12

3 **a** 35   **b** 84   **c** 120

4 53, 59

5 **a** 30 minutes   **b** 2.15 pm   **c** 3.30 pm

6 **a** $^2/_3$ **b** $^7/_8$ **c** $^1/_2$ **d** $^3/_8$ **e** $^2/_{15}$ **f** $^9/_{14}$

7 **a** $1^1/_2$ **b** $1^3/_4$ **c** $3^2/_3$ **d** $2^5/_6$ **e** $4^1/_5$ **f** $7^5/_8$

8 **a** $^5/_2$ **b** $^9/_4$ **c** $^{11}/_7$ **d** $^{15}/_4$ **e** $^{27}/_5$ **f** $^{91}/_8$

9 **a** $1^5/_{12}$ **b** $4^1/_8$ **c** $1^7/_{16}$ **d** $2^1/_6$ **e** $7^1/_3$ **f** $1^5/_9$

10 **a** $^{17}/_{64}$ in.   **b** $^7/_{32}$ in.

11 2.25

12 2.5

13 4.9

14 **a** 6   **b** 3

15 **a** 8 m   **b** 1 : 25   **c** 0.896 m^3

16 **a** 3^7 **b** 3^{16} **c** 3^5 **d** 3^7

17 **a** 5.32×10^6 **b** 2.376×10^2
  c 3×10^{-3} **d** 1.83×10^{-5}

18 **a** 40000 **b** 6340   **c** 0.196 **d** 0.000826

19 **a** 1.25×10^3 **b** 5×10^{-3}
  c 2.75×10^4 **d** 2.5×10^{-2}

20 **a** 3×10^5 km/s **b** 9 years

21 **a** 12 **b** -40 **c** 3 **d** 64 **e** 18 **f** 7

22 **a** $4x$ **b** $3x+10y$ **c** $6a-7b$
  d x^{10} **e** x^{-1} **f** x^4

23 **a** 10   **b** 5   **c** $2^2/_5$ **d** 3   **e** -2
  f 4   **g** 24 **h** 8   **i** 5

24 **a** $x=3, y=2$ **b** $x=6, y=-5$ **c** $x=7, y=5$

25 **a** $x = \frac{y+2}{3}$ **b** $x=3y+4$ **c** $x = \frac{2(s-ut)}{t^2}$

  d $x = \frac{uv}{u+v}$ **e** $x = \frac{2y+1}{y-1}$ **f** $x = \frac{gT^2}{4\pi^2}$

26 **a** x^2+5x+6 **b** y^2+2y-3 **c** $2x^2-9x-18$

27 **a** $(x+4)(x+1)$ **b** $(y-3)(y-2)$
  c $(x+3)(x-3)$ **d** $(a+5)(a-3)$
  e $(x-4)(x+1)$ **f** $(x+2)(x+10)$

28 32 p

29 **a** £480 **b** 8 weeks **c** $W = \frac{C-320}{80}$

30 **a** 2   **b** $-^2/_3$ **c** $-^6/_7$

31 **a** 2, 7   **b** 3, $-^5/_2$ **c** $-^3/_2, ^5/_2$

32 **a** $y=x+3$ **b** $y=8-2x$ **c** $y=^1/_3x+2^2/_3$

33 **a** 5   **b** 13   **c** 4.47 (2 dp)

34 **a** 33.7° **b** 59.3°   **c** 35.8°

35 **a** 6.55 cm   **b** 6.17 cm   **c** 6.88 m

36 **a** $AC = 7.6, BC = 7.9$ **b** 19.0

37 74.6°, 105.4°

38 15.4 cm

39 229.8

40 **a** 12.4 cm   **b** 598 cm^3

41 **a** 90°, 90°   **b** 1 : 3

42 **a** $\angle ORS$=90°, $\angle ORQ$=60°   **b** 30°, 30°
  c 21.7 cm^2

Exercise 2S   Skills Practice

1 **a** 11 **b** 4   **c** 20 **d** $^1/_2$ **e** $^2/_7$ **f** 3
  g $^1/_{10}$ **h** $^4/_3$ **i** $^3/_2$ **j** $^3/_4$ **k** $^{11}/_3$ **l** $^5/_2$

2 **a** x^7 **b** $6x^5y$ **c** $a^{7/4}$ **d** x^8
  e b^{-6} **f** m^6 **g** $45a^8b^2$ **h** $4x^3y^{-4}$
  i $y^{7/6}$ **j** $x^{27/10}$ **k** $625a^8b^4$ **l** $24x^{11/2}$
  m $7p^{3/2}$ **n** $5x^{5/2}$ **o** $30x^{-3}$ **p** $^1/_2x^2y^3$
  q $^3/_4x^{-5/2}$ **r** $108a^9b^8$

3 **a** 64 **b** 6   **c** 3   **d** 27 **e** 1   **f** 4
  g $^1/_2$ **h** $^3/_4$ **i** $^1/_4$ **j** $^1/_{243}$ **k** $^1/_2$ **l** $^5/_9$
  m 81 **n** $^8/_{27}$ **o** $^3/_2$ **p** $^1/_{16}$ **q** $^5/_4$ **r** $^3/_2$
  s 8   **t** 8   **u** -2 **v** $^2/_7$ **w** $^{243}/_{32}$ **x** -3

4 **a** $x^{1/2}$ **b** $5^{1/3}$ **c** $x^{1/5}$ **d** $10^{3/2}$ **e** $7^{3/2}$
  f $y^{3/2}$ **g** $a^{5/2}$ **h** 2^{-3} **i** y^{-4} **j** $b^{2/3}$
  k $b^{3/5}$ **l** $3x^{-1/2}$

5 **a** 2^{2x} **b** 2^{x+1} **c** 2^{6x} **d** 2^{6x-2} **e** 2^{x+2} **f** 2^{2x}

6   **a** $2\sqrt{3}$ **b** $3\sqrt{2}$ **c** $5\sqrt{2}$ **d** $2\sqrt{5}$ **e** $9\sqrt{2}$ **f** $7\sqrt{2}$
  g $6\sqrt{3}$ **h** $10\sqrt{10}$ **i** $11\sqrt{3}$ **j** $5\sqrt{3}$ **k** $\sqrt{5}$
  l $12\sqrt{3}$ **m** $17\sqrt{2}$ **n** $5\sqrt{7}$ **o** $16\sqrt{2}$

7   **a** $\sqrt{2}$ **b** $^1/_3\sqrt{3}$ **c** $^3/_4\sqrt{2}$
  d $^1/_3\sqrt{5}$ **e** $^2/_3\sqrt{3}$ **f** $^{12}/_{35}$

8   **a** $^3/_2$ **b** $^2/_5$ **c** 3 **d** 3 **e** $-^4/_7$ **f** $-^{12}/_5$

9   **a** $2+\sqrt{3}$ **b** $3\sqrt{2}-3$ **c** $\sqrt{6}-1$
  d $^1/_4(3+\sqrt{5})$ **e** $2-\sqrt{2}$ **f** $3+2\sqrt{2}$
  g $^1/_3(\sqrt{5}-1)$ **h** $^1/_{13}(5\sqrt{3}-6)$ **i** $^1/_3(4\sqrt{7}+7)$
  j $2+\sqrt{3}$ **k** $6-4\sqrt{2}$ **l** $^1/_6(15+11\sqrt{3})$
  m $^1/_4(11+7\sqrt{5})$ **n** $\sqrt{3}-2$ **o** $-67-47\sqrt{2}$

Exercise 2E   Exam Practice

1   **a i** 3^{5x+1} **ii** 3^{3x+6} **b** $^5/_2$

2   **b** $\sqrt{3}$

3   **a** $y = 6x - 2$

4 $3 + \sqrt{2}$

5 $\pi(52 + 22\sqrt{5})$

Exercise 3S   Skills Practice

1   **a** $(x+2)(x+1)$ **b** $(x+4)(x+1)$ **c** $(x+2)^2$
  d $(x+2)(x+4)$ **e** $(y+4)(y+9)$ **f** $(x-1)(x-3)$
  g $(x-5)(x-2)$ **h** $(x-10)(x-1)$
  i $(a+3)(a-1)$ **j** $(y+10)(y-6)$
  k $(x-3)(x+2)$ **l** $(p+5)(p+4)$ **m** $(x-6)(x+3)$
  n $(x+3)(x-3)$ **o** $(a-6)^2$ **p** $(m+7)(m-7)$
  q $(x+10)(x+7)$ **r** $(y+6)(y-5)$

2   **a** $-3, -1$ **b** 1 **c** $-7, 5$ **d** $1, 17$ **e** $-3, -4$
  f $-5, 9$ **g** $-9, 9$ **h** $-8, 7$ **i** $3, 12$

3   **a** $(2x+1)(x+1)$ **b** $(3y+1)(y-2)$
  c $(2x+3)(x+4)$ **d** $(5p-2)(p-2)$
  e $(6x+1)(x+1)$ **f** $(3y+1)(3y-1)$
  g $(4x-3)(x-1)$ **h** $(2a+1)^2$
  i $2(1+2x)(1-3x)$

4   **a** $-1, -^1/_5$ **b** $^1/_3, 5$ **c** $-^3/_2, 1$
  d $-3, 1$ **e** $-1, 4$ **f** $2, 4$
  g $-^3/_2, ^2/_5$ **h** $^1/_4, 2$ **i** $-^8/_3, -^5/_6$

5   **a** $(x+1)^2+2$ **b** $(x+4)^2-17$ **c** $(x-2)^2+1$
  d $(x+^3/_2)^2-^5/_4$ **e** $(x-^7/_2)^2-^{57}/_4$
  f $(x+8)^2-64$ **g** $(x+^1/_2)^2+^1/_4$
  h $(x-5)^2-22$ **i** $(x+^1/_3)^2+^1/_{18}$

6   **a** $2(x+1)^2-1$ **b** $3(x-^3/_2)^2-^{35}/_4$
  c $-(x-3)^2+13$ **d** $5(x+3)^2-64$
  e $2(x-^3/_4)^2+^{31}/_8$ **f** $6(x+^1/_{12})^2-^{25}/_{24}$
  g $-(x+^3/_2)^2+^{25}/_4$ **h** $4(x+^5/_2)^2-25$
  i $-2(x-^7/_4)^2+^{113}/_8$

7   **a** $-3, -1$ **b** $4, 10$ **c** $-1\pm\sqrt{2}$
  d $5\pm\sqrt{7}$ **e** $-3\pm^1/_2\sqrt{2}$ **f** $2\pm\sqrt{11}$

8   **a** $-19, 8$ **b** $-1, 3$ **c** $-1.43, -0.23$
  d $-0.47, 8.47$ **e** $-0.73, 0.59$ **f** $-1.31, 0.08$

9   **a** $7, 9$ **b** $^1/_6(-5\pm\sqrt{13})$ **c** $^1/_2(3\pm\sqrt{5})$
  d $1, ^{13}/_4$ **e** $4\pm^3/_2\sqrt{2}$ **f** $^1/_6(-5\pm\sqrt{145})$

10   **a** $-5, 2$ **b** $-^1/_2, 4$ **c** $\pm\sqrt{2}, \pm2\sqrt{2}$
  d $-^1/_5, ^1/_3$ **e** $1, ^9/_2$ **f** $-1, ^8/_3$

11   **a** -11, no real   **b** 32, real distinct
  c 44, real distinct **d** 0, real repeated
  e -23, no real   **f** 0, real repeated

12   **a** $(-8, 0), (-1, 0), (0, 8)$
  b $(-4, 0), (5, 0), (0, 20)$
  c $(-4.08, 0), (2.58, 0), (0, -21)$
  d $(0, 5)$ **e** $(-^5/_2, 0), (0, 0)$
  f $(-0.61, 0), (4.11, 0), (0, 5)$

13   **a** $(2, -1)$ min   **b** $(-1, 6)$ min
  c $(3, 16)$ max   **d** $(-3, -25)$ min
  e $(^9/_2, -^{21}/_4)$ min   **f** $(-^3/_2, ^{29}/_4)$ max

14   **a** $(-4, 0), (-2, 0), (0, 8), (-3, -1)$
  b $(-9, 0), (1, 0), (0, -9), (-4, -25)$
  c $(-2, 0), (3, 0), (0, -6), (^1/_2, -^{25}/_4)$
  d $(2, 0), (16, 0), (0, 32), (9, -49)$
  e $(-5, 0), (1, 0), (0, 5), (-2, 9)$
  f $(0, 12), (3, 3)$
  g $(0.38, 0), (2.62, 0), (0, 1), (^3/_2, -^5/_4)$
  h $(-4, 0), (0, 16)$
  i $(-5.37, 0), (0.37, 0), (0, 2), (-^5/_2, ^{33}/_4)$
  j $(^3/_2, 0), (3, 0), (0, 9), (^9/_4, -^9/_8)$
  k $(-0.94, 0), (0.94, 0), (0, -8)$
  l $(0, 3), (-^1/_{14}, ^{83}/_{28})$

Exercise 3E   Exam Practice

1   **a** $A = 2, B = ^3/_2, C = ^1/_2$ **b** $(-^3/_2, ^1/_2)$

2   **a** 2^{12x-6} **b** $3 \pm \sqrt{6}$

3   **a** $a = -28, b = 33$ **b** $(^{11}/_2, 0)$ **c** $(^7/_2, -16)$

4   **a** $1, 5$ **b** $1, 25$

5   **b** $-7, 17$

6 $-2 \pm \sqrt{2}$

7   **a** $x(2x - 3)(x - 6)$ **b** $0, ^3/_2, 6$

8   **a** $(0, -2), (0, -3)$ **b** $(y+^5/_2)^2-^1/_4; (-^1/_4, -^5/_2)$

9   **a** $8u^2 + 7u - 1 = 0$ **b** $^1/_2, -1$

10   **a** $(-2, 0), (-k, 0), (0, 2k)$ **b** $(-2, 0), (0, 4)$

11   **a i** t^2 **ii** $4t$ **b** 3

Exercise 4S   Skills Practice

1   **a** $(7, 11)$ **b** $(^4/_5, ^2/_5)$ **c** $(^1/_5, ^9/_5)$

2   **a** $(4, 1)$ **b** $(3, -2)$ **c** $(14, 5)$
  d $(7, -5)$ **e** $(-3, -3)$ **f** $(^1/_2, 6)$
  g $(9, -4)$ **h** $(^2/_3, 4)$ **i** $(^7/_2, ^3/_4)$

3   **a** $(1, 5), (3, 13)$ **b** $(-1, -3), (2, 0)$
  c $(^1/_2, 3), (2, -15)$

4   **a** $x=-4, y=-6; x=3, y=1$
  b $x=14, y=-6; x=0, y=1$
  c $x=-5, y=0; x=3, y=4$
  d $x=^1/_2, y=^{13}/_4; x=-2, y=7$
  e $x=3, y=1; x=5, y=-1$
  f $x=2, y=0; x=3, y=5$
  g $x=3, y=1; x=-3, y=-5$
  h $x=1, y=4; x=-2, y=5$
  i $x=3, y=^{12}/_5; x=^3/_2, y=3$

5   **a** $(-6, 8), (10, 0)$ **b** do not intersect
  c $(-^5/_3, -^2/_3), (2, 3)$ **d** $(4, 1), (-2, ^5/_2)$
  e $(-2, 3), (4, -5)$ **f** $(-^{20}/_{19}, -^{32}/_{19}), (1, -1)$

6   **a** $x=-2, y=-4; x=1, y=-1$ **b** $x=4, y=^1/_3$
  c $x=4, y=\pm1; x=-4, y=\pm1$

Exercise 4E   Exam Practice

1 $x=^1/_2, y=4; x=-^5/_8, y=-5$

2   **a** $(3, 1), (5, 5)$ **b** $2\sqrt{5}$

3   **a** $4p = 3q - 8$ **b** $p = -^{11}/_{16}, q = ^7/_4$

4 $a = ^1/_5, b = ^5/_2$

5   **b** $^{29}/_4$

6 $x = 3, y = ^1/_4$

Exercise 5S   Skills Practice

1   **a** $x < 5$ **b** $b \geq 2$ **c** $x > ^1/_2$ **d** $y \leq -2$
  e $x > ^8/_3$ **f** $x < 7$ **g** $a \geq ^{11}/_2$ **h** $x \leq -1$
  i $y > ^7/_4$ **j** $x > -9$ **k** $p \geq -^2/_5$ **l** $x \geq ^4/_3$

2   **a** $x > 5$ **b** $x \leq 2$ **c** $x < 8$ **d** $x \leq ^5/_2$
  e $x > 1$ **f** $x \leq -2$ **g** $x > 5$ **h** $x \leq ^3/_4$
  i $x < -3$ **j** $x \geq 8$ **k** $x < ^1/_5$ **l** $x < 1$
  m $x \leq ^2/_3$ **n** $x \geq -2$ **o** $x < -^4/_3$

3   **a** $3 < x < 5$ **b** $x < 3, x > 5$ **c** $-4 \leq x \leq ^1/_2$
  d $x < -5, x > -1$ **e** $a \leq -7, a \geq -3$
  f $1 < x < 2$ **g** $x \leq 0, x \geq 6$
  h $-3 \leq x \leq 2$ **i** $-3 < y < 6$
  j $a < -1, a > -^1/_2$ **k** $^1/_5 \leq x \leq 2$
  l $-12 < b < -9$ **m** $x \leq -1, x \geq -^2/_3$
  n $-18 < y < 3$ **o** $-5 \leq x \leq ^3/_2$

4   **a** $1-\sqrt{3} < x < 1+\sqrt{3}$
  b $y \leq ^1/_2(-3-\sqrt{5}), y \geq ^1/_2(-3+\sqrt{5})$
  c $x < 3-\sqrt{6}, x > 3+\sqrt{6}$
  d $b \leq ^1/_4(-1-\sqrt{33}), b \geq ^1/_4(-1+\sqrt{33})$
  e $x \leq 4-2\sqrt{5}, x \geq 4+2\sqrt{5}$
  f $^1/_{10}(-7-\sqrt{29}) \leq a \leq ^1/_{10}(-7+\sqrt{29})$

5   **a** $x < -5, x > -4$ **b** $-1 < x < 3$
  c $0.21 \leq x \leq 4.79$ **d** $x < -1.36, x > 0.86$
  e $x \leq ^3/_4, x \geq ^1/_2$ **f** $-2.30 < x < 1.30$
  g $x < 1, x > 8$ **h** $x \leq -^3/_2, x \geq 4$
  i $0.23 \leq x \leq 1.43$

6   **a** $x \leq 0, x \geq ^2/_3$
  b $-^4/_3 \leq x \leq ^3/_2$
  c $-2-2\sqrt{5} < b < -2+2\sqrt{5}$
  d $y \leq ^2/_5, y \geq ^7/_4$
  e $x < -10, x > 12$
  f $^1/_6(4-\sqrt{22}) \leq x \leq ^1/_6(4+\sqrt{22})$

Exercise 5E   Exam Practice

1   **a** $5, 8$ **b** $y \leq 5, y \geq 8$

2   **a** $x^2 + 16x \leq 192$ **b** $4x^2 > 100$
  c $5 < x \leq 8$

3 $^3/_2 < x < 5$

4   **b** $2 + 2\sqrt{3}$

Exercise 6S   Skills Practice

1   **a** $2x^3+3x^2+7x$ **b** $4x^5+5x^4+7x^3$
  c $6x^3-2x^2+3x$ **d** $x^4+2x^3-8x^2-2$
  e $x^8-3x^7-2x^6+6x^5$ **f** $14x^3-2x^2+x-1$
  g $x^2+8x-7+2x^{-1}$ **h** $6x^3-13x^2+2x$

2   **a** $6+6x+10x^2-7x^3-4x^5+4x^6$
  b $5-136x-5x^2+55x^3+2x^4$
  c $8x+5x^2+9x^3-x^4-2x^5+2x^6$
  d $6x^{-2}+x^{-1}+7-2x^3+9x^4$

3   **a** $x^4+6x^3+8x^2+8x+16$
  b $6x^4+11x^3-20x^2-55x+50$
  c $-3x^4+16x^3-7x^2+11x-5$
  d $2x^6-6x^5+3x^4-7x^3+4x^2+3x+6$
  e $x^4+4x^3+8x^2+13x+4$
  f $x^5-2x^4+11x^3-17x^2+44x-42$
  g $8x^5-30x^4-18x^3+43x^2+8x-15$
  h $8x^3+8x-2-6x^{-1}+5x^{-2}-x^{-3}$

4   **a** $A = 5, B = 1$ **b** $A = -2, B = 5$
  c $A = 3, B = 2$ **d** $A = 8, B = -4$
  e $A = 4, B = ^1/_2$ **f** $A = 1, B = 4$
  g $A = 9, B = -3$ **h** $A = 5, B = -4$
  i $A = -2, B = 7$ **j** $A = 4, B = 2$
  k $A = -4, B = -1$

5 **a** $A = 3, B = -1, C = 4$
b $A = 3, B = -1, C = 2$
c $A = 1, B = 4, C = 5$
d $A = 4, B = -6, C = 3$
e $A = -5, B = 3, C = 2$
f $A = 4, B = 1, C = -3$
g $A = -2, B = 2, C = 5$
h $A = 1, B = -2, C = -3$
i $A = 3, B = -{}^3/_2, C = -36{}^3/_4$
j $A = 5, B = 7, C = -6$
k $A = 1, B = -4, C = 4$
l $A = -1, B = 5, C = -2$

6 **a** x^2+3x+2 **b** $2x^2-5x+3$
c x^2+3x-4 r2   **d** x^2-x+6
e x^2+x-9 r28   **f** x^2-5x+7
g x^3+2x^2+3 **h** x^3+2x^2-x-7 r-21
i $2x^2+5x-4$ **j** $2x^3-x+1$ r1

7 **a** yes   **b** no   **c** yes

8 **a** no   **b** yes   **c** yes

9 **a** -6, 0, 24, 54; $(x+1)$
b 0, -6, 0, 24; $(x+2)(x-1)$
c 0, 3, 3, 0; $(x+2)(x-2)$
d 37, 0, 4, -3; $(x+1)$

10 **a** $(x-1)(x^2+2x+4)$ **b** $(x+2)(x+3)(x-3)$
c $(x-3)(x^2+5x+1)$ **d** $(x-2)(x-4)(x+1)$
e $(x-2)(2x-1)(x-3)$ **f** $(x+3)(3x+1)(x-4)$
g $(x-2)(x^2+2x+4)$ **h** $(1-x)(x^2-4x+1)$
i $(x-1)(x+1)(x^2+x+1)$

Exercise 6E   Exam Practice

1 **b** 1, 2, 5

2 $A = -2, B = -4, C = 10$

3 **b** $(x + 3)(2x + 3)(x - 2)$

4 **a** $(x^2 + 3)(x^2 - 2)$ **b** $\pm\sqrt{2}$

5 **a** $(x - 1)$ **b** $(2, 0), (4, 0)$

6 **a** 2

Exercise 7E   Exam Practice

1 **b** $(-4, 0), (-{}^1/_2, 0), (3, 0), (0, -12)$

2 $-2 \le x \le {}^5/_2$

3 **a** $4 + 3\sqrt{3}$ **b** $2\sqrt{5}$

4 $x = -1, y = -2; x = 5, y = 2$

5 **a** 4^{4x+2} **b** ${}^2/_3 \pm {}^1/_3\sqrt{10}$

6 **a** $A = -1, B = {}^3/_2, C = {}^{25}/_4$
b $(-{}^3/_2, {}^{25}/_4), (-4, 0), (1, 0), (0, 4)$

7 **a** $(-{}^1/_2, -2), (2, 3)$ **b** ${}^5/_2\sqrt{5}$

8 **a** 3   **b** -1.35, 1.85 (3 sf)

9 **a** $15\sqrt{2}$ **b** $1 + \sqrt{2}$

10 **a** $A = 1, B = -{}^5/_2, C = {}^3/_4$
b $A = 2, B = 4, C = -1$

11 **a** $(-1, 8), (4, -7)$

12 6 seconds

13 **a** $8 - 36x + 54x^2 - 27x^3$ **b** $170 - 117\sqrt{3}$

14 **a** 4, 9   **b** 8, 27

15 **a** $(x - \sqrt{2})^2 - 4$ **b** $(\sqrt{2}, -4)$
c $(\sqrt{2} - 2, 0), (\sqrt{2} + 2, 0)$

16 **a** 12 **b** $2x - 3$

17 **a** $1 < x < 6$ **b** 3.75

18 $x = -1, y = {}^3/_2$

Exercise 8S   Skills Practice

1 **a** 90°   **b** 60°   **c** 120°   **d** 15°
e 210° **f** 1440° **g** 20°   **h** 900°
i 225° **j** 420° **k** 67.5° **l** 810°

2 **a** 57.3°   **b** 229.2°   **c** 91.7°
d 20.1°   **e** 481.3°   **f** 62.5°

3 **a** 2π **b** ${}^\pi/_6$ **c** ${}^\pi/_4$ **d** ${}^{3\pi}/_4$ **e** ${}^{5\pi}/_3$ **f** ${}^\pi/_{18}$
g ${}^{3\pi}/_2$ **h** ${}^\pi/_9$ **i** 4π **j** ${}^{8\pi}/_3$ **k** ${}^\pi/_8$ **l** ${}^{15\pi}/_2$

4 **a** 0.87   **b** 4.36   **c** 0.59
d 3.42   **e** 0.32   **f** 12.39

5 **a** 5.2 cm **b** 14.5 cm

6 **a** 15.2 cm, 13.1 cm^2
b 57.5 cm, 205 cm^2
c 24.4 cm, 33.5 cm^2
d 240 cm, 3590 cm^2

7 **a** 1.53   **b** 3.95

8 **a** 7.8   **b** 9.4

Exercise 8E   Exam Practice

1 **a** 4 cm   **b** 0.44   **c** 18 cm^2

2 **a** 60π cm^2 **b** 36 cm^2 **c** 152.50 cm^2

3 **a** 37.0 cm (3 sf) **b** 53.6 cm^2 (3 sf)

4 **a** 1.43   **b** 18.2 cm^3

5 **a** 37.7 cm^2 **b** 22.1 cm^2 **c** 23.0 cm

6 **c** $18 + 2\sqrt{6}$

Exercise 9S   Skills Practice

1   **a** $\frac{1}{2}$ **b** $\frac{\sqrt{3}}{2}$ **c** 1 **d** $\frac{\sqrt{3}}{2}$ **e** $\sqrt{3}$
    f $-\frac{1}{\sqrt{2}}$ **g** 0 **h** 1 **i** $\frac{1}{\sqrt{3}}$ **j** $\frac{1}{2}$
    k $-\frac{1}{\sqrt{2}}$ **l** $-\frac{1}{\sqrt{3}}$ **m** $-\frac{1}{2}$ **n** $-\frac{1}{2}$ **o** $\sqrt{3}$
    p $\frac{1}{2}$ **q** $\frac{\sqrt{3}}{2}$ **r** 0 **s** $-\frac{1}{\sqrt{2}}$ **t** -1

2   **a** $\frac{1}{\sqrt{2}}$ **b** $\sqrt{3}$ **c** $\frac{\sqrt{3}}{2}$ **d** $\frac{\sqrt{3}}{2}$
    e 1 **f** $\frac{1}{2}$ **g** $\sqrt{3}$ **h** $-\frac{1}{\sqrt{2}}$
    i $-\frac{1}{\sqrt{3}}$ **j** $-\frac{1}{2}$ **k** $-\frac{\sqrt{3}}{2}$ **l** 0
    m $-\frac{1}{\sqrt{2}}$ **n** -1 **o** 0 **p** $\frac{1}{\sqrt{3}}$

3   **a** $(90, 1), (270, -1)$
    b $(90, 2), (270, -2)$
    c $(0, 3), (180, -3), (360, 3)$
    d $x=90, x=270$
    e $x=90, x=270$
    f $(0, \frac{1}{4}), (180, -\frac{1}{4}), (360, \frac{1}{4})$
    g $(45, 1), (135, -1), (225, 1), (315, -1)$
    h $x=180$
    i $(0, 2), (60, -2), (120, 2), (180, -2),$
       $(240, 2), (300, -2), (360, 2)$
    j $(90, -1), (270, 1)$
    k $(135, \frac{1}{2})$
    l $x=0, x=180, x=360$
    m $(150, -1), (330, 1)$
    n $(135, 4), (315, -4)$
    o $(0, 2), (180, 0), (360, 2)$
    p $x=90, x=270$

4   **a** $(0, 1), (\pi, -1), (2\pi, 1)$
    b $x=\frac{\pi}{4}, x=\frac{3\pi}{4}, x=\frac{5\pi}{4}, x=\frac{7\pi}{4}$
    c $(\frac{\pi}{3}, 1), (\frac{4\pi}{3}, -1)$
    d $x=\frac{3\pi}{4}, x=\frac{7\pi}{4}$
    e $(\frac{\pi}{6}, -2), (\frac{\pi}{2}, 2), (\frac{5\pi}{6}, -2), (\frac{7\pi}{6}, 2),$
       $(\frac{3\pi}{2}, -2), (\frac{11\pi}{6}, 2)$
    f $(0, \frac{5}{2}), (\pi, \frac{3}{2}), (2\pi, \frac{5}{2})$
    g $x=\frac{\pi}{2}, x=\frac{3\pi}{2}$
    h $(\frac{\pi}{4}, -3), (\frac{5\pi}{4}, 3)$

Exercise 9E   Exam Practice

1   **a** $p = 2, q = 3$ **b** $\frac{2\pi}{3}$ **c** $(\frac{2\pi}{3}, 2)$

2   **a** $-2 - \sqrt{3}$ **b** $2 + \sqrt{3}$

3   **a** $(\frac{\pi}{4}, 1), (\frac{3\pi}{4}, -1), (\frac{5\pi}{4}, 1), (\frac{7\pi}{4}, -1)$
    b $(\frac{2\pi}{3}, 2), (\frac{5\pi}{3}, 0)$

4   **a i** 90 **ii** $x = 180$
    b $0, 90, 180, 270, 360$

Exercise 10S   Skills Practice

1   **a** $30°, 150°$
    b $64.2°, 115.8°$
    c $200.5°, 339.5°$
    d $53.1°, 306.9°$
    e $90°, 270°$
    f $98.4°, 261.6°$
    g $20.8°, 200.8°$
    h $135°, 315°$
    i $105.2°, 285.2°$
    j $30°, 150°, 210°, 330°$
    k $22.5°, 112.5°, 202.5°, 292.5°$
    l $4.2°, 55.8°, 124.2°, 175.8°, 244.2°,$
       $295.8°$
    m $134.9°$
    n $105°, 165°, 285°, 345°$
    o $284.6°$
    p $19.6°, 100.4°$
    q $122.1°, 327.9°$
    r $131.6°, 311.6°$
    s $187.5°, 352.5°$
    t $34.9°, 214.9°$
    u $51.2°, 176.8°$

2   **a** $-108.3°, 71.7°$
    b $-174.7°, -95.3°, 5.3°, 84.7°$
    c $-180°, -60°, 60°, 180°$
    d $-133.1°, -46.9°$
    e $-180°, -135°, -90°, -45°, 0°, 45°, 90°,$
       $135°, 180°$
    f $-83.3°, -28.7°$
    g $35.5°, 144.5°$
    h $-21.8°, 158.2°$
    i $-63.6°, 63.6°$
    j $-162.5°, 17.5°$
    k $-40.2°, 70.2°$
    l $-68.3°, -21.7°, 111.7°, 158.3°$

3   **a** $0.67, 3.82$ **b** $1.88, 4.40$
    c $1.27, 1.87$ **d** $0.84, 5.44$
    e 4.71 **f** $1.44, 4.58$
    g $0.54, 2.10$ **h** $3.37, 5.01$
    i $1.70, 4.84$
    j $0.74, 2.40, 3.88, 5.55$
    k $0.79, 1.83, 2.88, 3.93, 4.97, 6.02$
    l $1.21, 3.50$

4   **a** $\frac{\pi}{6}, \frac{5\pi}{6}$ **b** $\frac{\pi}{6}, \frac{11\pi}{6}$
    c $0, \pi, 2\pi$ **d** $\frac{2\pi}{3}, \frac{4\pi}{3}$
    e $\frac{\pi}{4}, \frac{3\pi}{4}$ **f** $\frac{\pi}{3}, \frac{4\pi}{3}$
    g $\frac{\pi}{6}, \frac{\pi}{3}, \frac{7\pi}{6}, \frac{4\pi}{3}$ **h** $\frac{5\pi}{12}, \frac{17\pi}{12}$
    i $\frac{3\pi}{2}$ **j** $0, \frac{4\pi}{3}, 2\pi$
    k $\frac{\pi}{18}, \frac{7\pi}{18}, \frac{13\pi}{18}, \frac{19\pi}{18}, \frac{25\pi}{18}, \frac{31\pi}{18},$
    l $0, \frac{\pi}{2}, 2\pi$

5 **a** 37.5°, 97.5°, 217.5°, 277.5°
    b 40.9°, 169.1°, 220.9°, 349.1°
    c 27.8°, 87.8°, 147.8°, 207.8°, 267.8°,
       327.8°
    d 19.5°, 160.5°
    e 48.2°, 131.8°, 228.2°, 311.8°
    f 53.1°, 126.9°, 233.1°, 306.9°
    g 32.6°, 57.4°, 122.6°, 147.4°, 212.6°,
       237.4°, 302.6°, 327.4°
    h 45°, 108.4°, 225°, 288.4°
    i 116.6°, 135°, 296.6°, 315°
    j 60°, 90°, 270°, 300°
    k 90°, 210°, 330°
    l 63.4°, 161.6°, 243.4°, 341.6°
    m 0°, 120°, 180°, 240°, 360°
    n 0°, 41.8°, 138.2°, 180°, 360°
    o 75.5°, 284.5°
    p 78.7°, 135°, 258.7°, 315°

6 **a** $y/_r$ **b** $x/_r$ **c** $y/_x$

8 **a** 63.4°, 243.4°
    b 26.6°, 153.4°, 206.6°, 333.4°
    c 0°, 180°, 210°, 330°, 360°
    d 78.5°, 180°, 281.5°
    e 108.4°, 288.4°
    f 19.5°, 160.5°
    g 65.9°, 114.1°, 245.9°, 294.1°
    h 30°, 150°

9 **a** $-{}^{11\pi}/_{12}, -{}^{\pi}/_4, {}^{\pi}/_{12}, {}^{3\pi}/_4$
    b 3.02
    c -2.16, -0.98, 0.98, 2.16
    d $-{}^{\pi}/_2$, -0.84, 0.84, ${}^{\pi}/_2$
    e ${}^{\pi}/_2$
    f $-{}^{3\pi}/_4$, -0.67, ${}^{\pi}/_4$, 2.47
    g -1.85, 1.29
    h 0.73, 2.41
    i $-\pi, \pi$
    j $-\pi$, -2.27, $-{}^{\pi}/_2$, -0.87, 0, 0.87, ${}^{\pi}/_2$, 2.27, π

Exercise 10E   Exam Practice

1 **a** $-{}^{5\pi}/_8, {}^{\pi}/_8, {}^{3\pi}/_8, {}^{7\pi}/_8$ **b** $-{}^{\pi}/_2, -{}^{\pi}/_6$

2 **a** (90, 4), (270, -2)
    b (199.5, 0), (340.5, 0)

3 **a** -180°, 60°, 180°   **b** 30°, 90°, 150°

4 **a** $(0, {}^{\sqrt3}/_2)$ **b** (15, 1)   **c** (60, 0)

5 **a** ${}^{\pi}/_3, {}^{2\pi}/_3, {}^{4\pi}/_3, {}^{5\pi}/_3$ **b** ${}^{\pi}/_4, {}^{5\pi}/_4$

6 **a** 4   **b** $(0, -2\sqrt3)$, (60, 0), (240, 0)

Exercise 11E   Exam Practice

1 **a** 60°, 150°   **b** 60°, 120°, 240°, 300°

2 **a** 1.42   **b** 19.4

3 **a** -0.7808, 1.281 **b** -0.896, -2.25 (3 sf)

4 **b** $5 < r < 10$

5 **b** -120°, -90°, 90°, 120°

6 **a** ${}^2/_3(\pi - 1)$

7 **a** ${}^1/_{\sqrt2}$ **b** ${}^{3\pi}/_8, {}^{7\pi}/_8, {}^{11\pi}/_8, {}^{15\pi}/_8$

8 **a** ${}^3/_4$, 2   **b** 36.9°, 63.4°, 216.9°, 243.4°

9 **a** (0, -2)   **b** (180, 4)   **c** 70.5, 289.5

10 $2 + \sqrt3$

11 **a** 4   **b** ${}^1/_3$

12 **b** $96(2\pi + 3\sqrt3)$

13 **b** 0, ${}^{\pi}/_3$, π, ${}^{5\pi}/_3$, 2π

14 **a** 120°   **c** (60, 0), (100, 0)

Exercise 12S   Skills Practice

1 **a** 4, 7, 10, 13, 16   **b** 1, 7, 13, 19, 25
    c -17, -6, 5, 16, 27 **d** 21, 17, 13, 9, 5
    e 5, 6.5, 8, 9.5, 11
    f -10, -25, -40, -55, -70

2 **a** $2n+5$ **b** $4n-2$ **c** $42-7n$
    d $5n-17$ **e** $30-13n$ **f** $0.8n-0.4$

3 **a** 25, 55   **b** 38, 98   **c** -28, -133
    d 33, 108 **e** -100, -295 **f** 7.6, 19.6

4 **a** 12, 27   **b** 15   **c** $3(n-1)^2$ **d** $6n-3$

5 $31-12n$

6 **a** 320   **b** 77

7 **a** 140   **b** 6705   **c** 336

8 **a** 35   **b** 7   **c** 33

9 **a** 4270   **b** 133   **c** 6963

10 **a** 48   **b** 915   **c** 2091
    d 319   **e** 1496   **f** -1122

11 **a** ${}^7/_4n+{}^3/_4$ **b** 382.5

12 **a** 5050   **b** 1050   **c** 4000

13 30000

14 **a** 3   **b** 175

15 a 22, 4.5   b 95

16 a 19, -4   b $21n-2n^2$

17 a 2, 8   b 2652

18 a $^1/_2$, $^{15}/_2$ b 17

Exercise 12E   Exam Practice

1 a -11, 4   b 4350

2 b 23

3 a i $38 - 5k$ ii $760 + 90k$ b 31.5

4 a 8   b 7, 12

5 a 3, 14   b $7n^2 - 4n$

6 a 3225   b 19

Exercise 13S   Skills Practice

1 a 3, 9, 27, 81   b 7, 49, 343, 2401
  c -4, 16, -64, 256   d 6, 12, 24, 48
  e 1, 6, 36, 216   f $^2/_3$, $^4/_9$, $^8/_{27}$, $^{16}/_{81}$

2 a 5^n b $(^1/_2)^n$ c 4×3^n
  d $(-2)^n$ e $36 \times (^1/_3)^n$ f 2^{n-2}

3 a 1275   b -1641   c 191.8125

4 a 2, 6, 14   b 2, 4, 8   c 64

5 648

6 a 5115   b 269.96   c -2724.74

7 a 20   b 2400   c 52.57

8 a 131100   b 354300   c 0.9961
  d 19530   e 88560   f 82.87

9 a $2 \times (^3/_2)^{n-1}$ b $r > 1$

10 a $^5/_8$ b 37.62

11 a $-^1/_6$ b $^7/_{36}$

12 a $^1/_2$ b 160

13 a 5, -3   b 24605

14 a 22000   b 26620   c 46.41%

15 a £5955.08   b £2969.24

16 a -54, $-^2/_3$ b -32.4

Exercise 13E   Exam Practice

1 a $\pm \, ^1/_6$ b 777.6, -555.4

2 a £4305   b 42000

3 a $1 + \sqrt{3}$ b $7 + 4\sqrt{3}$

4 a 8   b $62^1/_2$

5 b 90.6 m

6 a $^k/_2$ b $\frac{32}{k^2}$ c 342

Exercise 14E   Exam Practice

1 a -9, 4   b 6540

2 a 54, $^2/_3$ b 162

3 b £543000

4 a $83 - 4n$ b 20   c 820

5 a $^1/_3\sqrt{3}$ b $^4/_{27}$

6 a $^2/_3$

7 a $2x - 3$ b $8x - 6$ c $56x - 36$

8 a 67.03   b 7350

9 b $8\sqrt{2} - 10$

10 a -6   b 16

11 b £5310.78

Exercise 15S   Skills Practice

1 a $(y-3)=2(x-4)$ b $y=^1/_2(x-5)$
  c $(y-6)=3(x+1)$ d $(y-5)=(x+5)$
  e $(y-^5/_2)=-4(x-8)$ f $(y+2)=^3/_4(x+7)$

2 a $y=3x+6$ b $y=x$ c $y=-2x+17$
  d $y=^1/_3x+10$ e $y=5x-^7/_2$ f $y=-^1/_2x-4$

3 a $x-y-4=0$ b $2x+y-42=0$
  c $x+y=0$ d $3x-y-13=0$
  e $x-4y+10=0$ f $3x+5y+57=0$

4 a $y=x+4$ b $y=^1/_2x+5$ c $y=2x-5$
  d $y=^2/_3x+2$ e $y=-2x+8$ f $y=-^1/_5x-^{17}/_{20}$

5 a $x-y-8=0$ b $x+y+2=0$
  c $2x-3y+8=0$ d $x-8y-3=0$
  e $5x-2y+8=0$ f $4x+5y+21=0$

6 a 1   b -3   c 5   d -3   e $^1/_2$
  f -1   g $^7/_2$ h $-^1/_5$ i $-^8/_5$

7 b and d

8 a and f; c and h

9 **a** $y=3x-1$ **b** $y=-x+4$
    c $y=^2/_3x+6$ **d** $y=-^1/_4x+^{13}/_4$

10 **a** $x+2y-11=0$ **b** $x-3y-3=0$
    c $2x+3y-22=0$ **d** $4x-5y-39=0$

11 **a** $(4, 2)$ **b** $(6, 5)$ **c** $(^5/_2, 10)$
    d $(-2, 7)$ **e** $(-^3/_2, ^1/_2)$ **f** $(^{17}/_4, -^1/_2)$

12 **a** $x+y-4=0$ **b** $2x+y-3=0$
    c $x+2y-8=0$ **d** $2x-3y+11=0$
    e $4x+3y-4=0$ **f** $10x+12y-39=0$

13 **a** $y=2x+6$ **b** $(0,6), (-3, 0)$

14 **a** $y=-4x+13$ **b** $y=-4x-21$

15 **a** $x-2y+8=0$ **b** $(-4, 2)$ **c** $2\sqrt{5}$

16 **a** $y=-2x+10$ **b** $(0, 10), (5, 0)$ **c** 25

17 **a** $2x-3y+13=0$ **b** $3x+2y-13=0$ **c** $(1, 5)$

Exercise 15E   Exam Practice

1 **a** $2x - 3y + 10 = 0$ **b** $y = 2x - 12$
    c $(5, -2)$

2 **a** $(^{17}/_2, 0)$ **b** $(^1/_2, 2)$ **c** $^{17}/_2$

3 **a** $x + 2y - 35 = 0$ **b** $(7, 14)$

4 **a** $3x - 4y + 18 = 0$ **b** 18

5 **a** $y = 3x + 9$ **b** $6x - 2y + 21 = 0$

Exercise 16S   Skills Practice

1 **a** $2x$ **b** $7x^6$ **c** $4x^3$ **d** $-2x^{-3}$
    e $-5x^{-6}$ **f** 1   **g** 0   **h** 5
    i $8x$ **j** $6x^2$ **k** $-24x^{-5}$ **l** $-24x^{-4}$

2 **a** $3t^2$ **b** 10   **c** $-2t^{-2}$ **d** 0
    e $^1/_2t^{-1/2}$ **f** $10t^{3/2}$ **g** $-3t^{-3/2}$ **h** $^9/_2t^{1/2}$
    i $6t^{-1/3}$ **j** $-^{15}/_4t^{-7/4}$ **k** $^2/_3t^{1/3}$ **l** $2t^{1/5}$

3 **a** $3x^2+10x$ **b** $8x^3-3$
    c $8-12x^{-4}$ **d** $7x^6+30x^4-3x^2$
    e $3x^2-3$ **f** $2x-4$
    g $6x+20$ **h** $4x-17$
    i $9+2x^{-1/2}$ **j** $15x^{3/2}+x^{-2}$
    k $8x^{1/3}-^2/_3x^{-2/3}$ **l** $-x^{-3}-^7/_3x^{-9/2}$

4 **a** $-3x^{-2}$ **b** $-^1/_3x^{-2}$ **c** $^1/_2x^{-1/2}$
    d $-3x^{-3/2}$ **e** $^1/_3x^{-2/3}$ **f** $^3/_2x^{1/2}$

5 **a** $36x-1$ **b** $3x^2+4-6x^{-3}$
    c $2x+8$ **d** $4x^3-4x-15x^{-4}$
    e $10x^4-6$ **f** $3x^2-10x+6$
    g $3x^2-4x-3$ **h** $2x^{-1/2}$
    i $6x+x^{-2}$ **j** $-6x^{-3}+^1/_4x^{-3/2}$
    k $^3/_2x^{1/2}-^3/_2x^{-1/2}$ **l** $6x^{-2/3}-2x^2$

6 **a** $12x^2$ **b** $6x-14$ **c** $-2x^{-3}+18x^{-4}$
    d $12x^2-12$ **e** $3x^{-1/2}+^3/_2x^{-5/2}$ **f** $^3/_8x^{-5/2}$

7 **a** 12   **b** 3   **c** $^5/_2$

8 **a** 6   **b** 0   **c** 5

9 **a** $y=2x-1$ **b** $y=7x-16$ **c** $y=-6$
    d $y=-10x+29$ **e** $x-4y+16=0$ **f** $3x-2y-4=0$

10 **a** $x+4y-18=0$ **b** $x+y-6=0$
    c $x+2y-5=0$ **d** $x-8y+124=0$
    e $4x+6y+19=0$ **f** $3x+4y-75=0$

11 **a** $-^3/_2$ **b** ±3 **c** $-2, 1$
    d ±2 **e** $0, ^4/_3$ **f** $-^2/_3, 2$

12 **a** $x > ^3/_2$ **b** $x < 0, x > 2$ **c** $x < -5, x > -1$

13 **a** $-^1/_3 < t < ^1/_3$ **b** $-1 < t < 7$ **c** $t < 0, t > ^2/_3$

14 **a** $(-2, -5)$ **b** $(-2, -5)$

15 **a** $(-1, -9)$, min   **b** $(^5/_2, ^3/_4)$, min
    c $(-2, 16)$, max; $(2, -16)$, min
    d $(0, 6)$, min; $(2, 10)$, max
    e $(0, 4)$, pt. infl.
    f $(0, 0)$, min; $(1, 1)$, max; $(2, 0)$, min
    g $(-^1/_2, -4)$, max; $(^1/_2, 4)$, min
    h $(9, 9)$, max   **i** $(-^1/_2, -12)$, max

16 **a** $(-1, 4), (1, -8)$ **b** $(-5, 75), (^1/_3, -^{23}/_{27})$
    c $(-2, -27), (4, 81)$

17 **a** $2x-6$ **b** $x-2y-20=0$

18 **a** 3 m/s   **b** $^{16}/_5$ m

19 **a** $3x^2-4x+3$ **b** $(^1/_3, 5^{22}/_{27}), (1, 7)$

20 **b** $36x-x^2$

21 **a** $(0, 0), (4, 0)$ **b** $y=4x$ **c** $y=-4x+16$

22 **a** 0   **b** $(-3, -6)$, max; $(3, 6)$, min

23 **a** $-^5/_3$ cm/s   **b** $^{13}/_4$

Exercise 16E   Exam Practice

1 **a** $y = -5x + 10$ **b** $y = 3x + 2$ **c** $(1, 5)$

2 **a** $(-3, 0), (-^3/_4, 0)$ **b** $(-^3/_2, 3), (^3/_2, 27)$

3 **a** $h = \dfrac{1000}{r^2}$ **c** 300π

4 **a** -3 **b** $^1/_3(1 - \sqrt{10}) < x < ^1/_3(1 + \sqrt{10})$

5 **a** $(-^3/_2, 0)$ **b** $6x - 8y + 9 = 0$

6 **a** $(15 + 12h - 3h^2)$ /hr **c** 450 /min

7 **a** $^5/_2r^2\theta$ cm^2 **c** $^2/_5, 8\sqrt{10}$

Exercise 17S   Skills Practice

1 **a** $\frac{1}{3}x^3+c$ **b** $\frac{1}{9}x^9+c$ **c** $\frac{1}{6}x^6+c$
   d $-x^{-1}+c$ **e** $\frac{1}{2}x^2+c$ **f** $4x+c$
   g $-\frac{1}{4}x^{-4}+c$ **h** x^3+c **i** $-4x^{-2}+c$
   j $\frac{2}{5}x^5+c$ **k** $-3x^{-1}+c$ **l** $\frac{7}{4}x^4+c$
   m $\frac{2}{3}x^{3/2}+c$ **n** $\frac{3}{4}x^{4/3}+c$ **o** $4x^{1/4}+c$
   p $3x^{5/3}+c$ **q** $\frac{15}{2}x^{2/5}+c$ **r** $2x^{1/6}+c$

2 **a** $\frac{1}{4}r^4+c$ **b** $2r^2+c$ **c** $-\frac{2}{5}r^{-5}+c$
   d $19r+c$ **e** $\frac{3}{11}r^{11/3}+c$ **f** $\frac{5}{2}r^{4/5}+c$
   g $\frac{2}{3}r^{3/2}+c$ **h** $-r^{-1}+c$ **i** $-r^{-3}+c$
   j $r^{1/2}+c$ **k** $\frac{3}{5}r^{5/3}+c$ **l** $\frac{20}{3}r^{3/4}+c$

3 **a** x^3-5x^2+c **b** $2x^4+2x+c$
   c $3x^5+2x^3-4x+c$ **d** $7x-\frac{1}{3}x^3+c$
   e $x^4+\frac{2}{3}x^3-x+c$ **f** $2x^3+\frac{5}{2}x^2+3x+c$
   g $3x^2-x^{-1}+c$ **h** $\frac{1}{6}x^6-\frac{1}{4}x^4-3x^{-3}+c$
   i $\frac{1}{3}x^3+\frac{3}{2}x^2+c$ **j** $\frac{1}{3}x^3-\frac{5}{2}x^2+4x+c$
   k $\frac{1}{2}x^6+x^{-2}+c$ **l** $\frac{1}{4}x^4-2x^3+6x^2-8x+c$

4 **a** $\frac{8}{3}x^3+\frac{1}{2}x^2-x+c$ **b** $\frac{1}{2}t^4+\frac{1}{3}t^3+\frac{1}{2}t^2+c$
   c $\frac{1}{3}x^3+2x^2+4x+c$ **d** $\frac{2}{5}x^{5/2}+\frac{2}{3}x^{3/2}+c$
   e $\frac{1}{8}x^4-\frac{1}{5}x^5+c$ **f** $\frac{1}{4}r^4+r^3-\frac{1}{2}r^2-3r+c$
   g $\frac{6}{7}x^{7/3}-\frac{15}{4}x^{4/3}+c$ **h** $2x^{1/2}-3x^{-2}+c$
   i $4x^{-2}\frac{3}{3}x^{3/2}+c$ **j** $6y^{7/2}-\frac{3}{2}y^2+c$
   k $\frac{1}{6}x^3+2x+c$ **l** $\frac{2}{15}x^5+\frac{1}{6}x^2+2x^{-1}+c$

5 **a** $y=x^2+3x-7$ **b** $y=x^3-2x^2+3x-3$
   c $y=\frac{1}{4}x^4-6x^{-2}+\frac{1}{2}$

6 **a** $4x^2-7x+5$ **b** x^3-2x-7
   c $12+x-4x^2-x^3$ **d** $\frac{1}{2}x^4-\frac{9}{2}x^2+6x-6$
   e $2x^{3/2}-4x^{1/2}+5$ **f** x^3-4x^2-3x-2

7 **a** 48 **b** -4 **c** 9 **d** 18 **e** 48 **f** $^{34}/_3$
   g 1 **h** 177 **i** $-^{23}/_{30}$

8 6

9 **a** -22 **b** 22

10 **a** (0, 0), (4, 0) **b** $^{32}/_3$

11 **a** 108 **b** $^4/_3$ **c** $^{27}/_4$

12 **a** (0, 1), (2, 1) **b** 4

13 **a** (-1, 6), (3, 10) **b** $^{32}/_3$

14 **a** $^4/_3$ **b** 4 **c** 9

15 **a** (0, 1), (0, 4) **b** $^9/_2$

16 **a** $^4/_3$ **b** $62\frac{1}{2}$ **c** $5^5/_{24}$

17 **a** $^7/_6$ **b** $21\frac{1}{6}$

Exercise 17E   Exam Practice

1 **a** $2x^4+x^2-6$ **b** $^{52}/_{15}$

2 **a** (-1, 33), (3, 1) **b** $^{45}/_4$

3 **a** $4x^{3/2}-2x^{1/2}+c$ **b** $-2+10\sqrt{3}$

4 **a** (4, 2), (4, 5) **b** $^9/_2$

5 **a** $x+8-2x^{-1}$ **b** $-4\pm3\sqrt{2}$

6 **a** $y=27-3x$ **b** $22\frac{1}{2}$

7 **a** 1, 4 **b** (1, 0), (4, 0) **c** $^1/_2$

8 **a** $y=\frac{1}{2}x+1$ **b** $(^1/_2, ^5/_4)$

Exercise 18E   Exam Practice

1 $-8<x<2$

2 **a** $8x^2-x^{-2}+c$ **b** $8x^2-x^{-2}+7$

3 **a** $y=2x-12$ **b** $4\sqrt{5}$

4 **a** (0, 0), (2, 2) **b** $^8/_3$

5 **a** $\pm^k/_3$ **b** $(-\frac{k}{3}, \frac{11k^3}{9})$, $(\frac{k}{3}, \frac{7k^3}{9})$

6 **a** $x^3-10x^{3/2}+25$ **b** $^{59}/_4$

7 **a** $y=3-3x$ **b** $y=x$ **c** $(^3/_4, ^3/_4)$

8 **b** $(2+\sqrt{3}, 1+2\sqrt{3})$ **c** $112-64\sqrt{3}$

9 **a** (9, 9) **b** $43\frac{1}{2}$

10 **b** $\sqrt{10}$ **c** $90°$

11 **a** $l=\frac{25\sqrt{3}}{x}-\frac{\sqrt{3}x}{3}$ **c** 250

12 **a** (14, -1) **b** $y=27-2x$
    c $y=x-3$ **d** (10, 7)

13 **a** $x+2y-33=0$

Exercise 19S   Skills Practice

(All Proof)

Exercise 19E   Exam Practice

3   **b** 3

4   **a** $x + 8y - 26 = 0$

5   **b** $p = 1, q = 1$ **c** $1 \pm \frac{1}{2}\sqrt{2}$

6   **b** $\frac{\pi}{4}, \frac{3\pi}{4}, \frac{5\pi}{4}, \frac{7\pi}{4}$

7   **b** $6 \pm 3\sqrt{5}$

8   **b** $(-a, 0)$

9   **b** 216.8

10 **a** $b^2 - 4ac \geq 0$

12 **a** $\frac{1}{2}n(n + 1)a + nb$

Exercise 20E   Exam Practice

1 $-\frac{1}{3} < y < 4$

2   **b** $(x - 2)^2(3x + 1)$ **c** $9x^2 - 22x + 8$
       d $\frac{4}{9}, 2$

3   **a** 5   **b** 0.28   **c** $y = 7 - x$

5   **a** 3   **b** 3   **c** π

7   **b** £41593

8   **a** 23.6°, 156.4° (1 dp)
       c $23.6 < x < 156.4$

9   **a** $(-1, 0)$

10 **a** $(2a - 1)(b + 1)$ **b** $\frac{\pi}{3}, \frac{3\pi}{2}, \frac{5\pi}{3}$

11 **a** $\sqrt{10}$ **b** 5   **c** $y = 3x - 9$
       d $x + 3y - 8 = 0$

12 **a** πr

13 **a** $9 + 2\sqrt{3}$ **b** $6 + 10\sqrt{3}$

14 $a = -3, b = 2; a = 3, b = -2$

15 **a** $4p^2 + p^{-2}$
       b $4p^4 - 20p^2 + 13 + 30p^{-2} + 9p^{-4}$

16 **a** 1, 2

17 **a** $\frac{15}{2}x^{1/2}(x - 1)$ **b** $(1, -2)$

18 **b** $(\frac{\pi}{8}, \frac{1}{\sqrt{2}}), (\frac{5\pi}{8}, -\frac{1}{\sqrt{2}}), (\frac{9\pi}{8}, \frac{1}{\sqrt{2}}),$
       $(\frac{13\pi}{8}, -\frac{1}{\sqrt{2}})$

19 **b** $-1 \leq k \leq 3$

20 **a** $(x - 1)(x + 2)(2x + 3)$ **b** $-1.76, 0.0946$

21 $(-2, 1), (1, 4)$

22 **b** 4   **c** 15, 60, 105, 150

23 $\frac{16}{81}, \frac{81}{16}$

24 **a** $(2x - 3)^2 + 2$ **b** $(\frac{3}{2}, 2)$

25 **a** $(0, 2), (2, 2)$ **b** $\frac{16}{3}$

26 $x < -2, x > 2$

27 **a** geometric   **b** $-1 < r < 1$ **c** $\frac{7}{33}$

29 **b** $x + 2y + 4 = 0$ **c** $(-3, -\frac{1}{2})$

30 **a** $(x - \frac{5}{2})^2 + \frac{3}{4}$ **b** $\frac{4}{3}$

31 **a** $k^2 - k$ **b** -2   **c** 162

32 **a** $\sin x = \frac{1}{2}, \cos y = -\frac{1}{2}$
       b $x = 30, y = 120; x = 150, y = 120$

33 **b** $8x^3 - 12x^2 + 6x - 2$ **d** $\frac{1}{2}$

34 **a** $\sqrt{2}r$

35 $\frac{3}{2}$

36 **b** $p = -\frac{1}{3}, q = -9; p = -3, q = -1$

37 **b** 22